The Second Wave

BRITISH DRAMA OF THE SIXTIES

Now re-issued with a revised and updated bibliography, *The Second Wave* is John Russell Taylor's sequel to *Anger and After*. His investigation includes detailed assessments of the work of Edward Bond, Tom Stoppard, Peter Terson, Peter Nichols, David Storey, Joe Orton, David Mercer and Charles Wood – the key figures of the Second Wave. Along with these he looks at the work of many other dramatists writing in the sixties, some of them young or little known then, many of whom are leading lights in the theatre of the 1970's – among them Alan Ayckbourn, Simon Gray and Howard Brenton.

This is an indispensable account of a period in British theatre when the challenge to the established order which John Russell Taylor wrote about in *Anger and After* had given a new generation of young writers the impetus to break further new ground, and the freedom to experiment, even to change the whole conception of theatre as it was then known. The book not only makes fascinating reading in its own right but also provides invaluable background material for anyone wanting to understand the achievements which lie behind the theatre of the 1970's.

'*The Second Wave*, with its clear capsule judgments on current work, is a useful book now, and will get more and more useful as the age it so sharply portrays recedes into the past.' B. A. Young, *The Financial Times by the same author*

Anger and After
Cinema Eye, Cinema Ear
The Penguin Dictionary of the Theatre
The Art Nouveau Book in Britain
The Rise and Fall of the Well-Made Play
Directors and Directions

JOHN RUSSELL TAYLOR

The Second Wave

BRITISH DRAMA OF THE SIXTIES

EYRE METHUEN · LONDON

First published in hardback by Methuen & Co Ltd 1971
Reprinted in paperback with new bibliography 1978
by Eyre Methuen Ltd,
11 New Fetter Lane, London EC4P 4EE
Copyright © 1971, 1978 by John Russell Taylor
Printed in Great Britain
by Cox & Wyman Ltd
Fakenham, Norfolk

ISBN 0 413 45440 1

Contents

Newer than New

It is one of the little oddities of English life – lovable, foreigners sometimes say – that topographically anything labelled 'new' – New Bridge, New Road, New College – can be relied upon to turn out as the oldest in the place. Few traditions, indeed, are more religiously adhered to than the tradition of the new; once the label has been affixed, nothing on earth seems able to remove it. And so it looks like becoming with the New Drama – the product of that famous dramatic revolution in Britain which began on May 8 1956 with the opening of John Osborne's *Look Back in Anger* at the Royal Court. It caused, of course, a surge of journalistic excitement in which the term 'the New Drama' took its place in our everyday vocabulary along with 'angry young man', 'theatre of the absurd', 'theatre of cruelty', 'comedy of menace' and others such. And when, almost at once, the purely journalistic excitement began to subside – before we knew for sure where this New Drama was coming from and what it was, people began asking in print where it was going and where it had gone – the term remained, like a fossil left on the shore by a retreating tide. So it looks, for the moment, as though we are stuck with it; perhaps, like *l'art nouveau*, it is with us for ever.

Before we take it as read, though, we should perhaps ask ourselves if it is not in itself question-begging, and always was. Is there, has there ever been, any such thing as *the* New Drama? New dramas there have certainly been, by the hundred, in the last fifteen years, and new dramatists too. But it became evident almost at once that they did not add up to a movement, and did not for that matter show any signs of wanting to. The revolution, if revolution there had been, was much more importantly a revolution in the theatre than a revolution in drama. Of course, the one inevitably produced symptoms of the other, but the symptoms should not too readily be taken for the disease. Some of the new dramatists were naturally novel, some caught novelty, and some had novelty thrust upon them. And some took no notice of the whole business, but just went on in their sweet old-fashioned way, as if nothing had happened.

But then, what exactly had happened? *Look Back in Anger* had been produced. But it was hardly a revolutionary sort of drama; indeed, as Osborne himself observed a little later, it was 'a formal, rather old-fashioned play' cast in an easily recognizable realistic mould, and with only a certain unfamiliarity of tone (the 'angry young man' tone) to distinguish it from many plays which had gone before. Nor did it found a school of social-protest drama; any expectations of that kind were rapidly knocked on the head by the next arrivals among new dramatists. Ann Jellicoe, N. F. Simpson, John Arden, Harold Pinter might be given many labels, but 'social realists' and 'playwrights of protest' would hardly be among them. True, Osborne was only 26 when *Look Back in Anger* was staged, but youthful playwrights were no absolute novelty in even the relatively recent history of English drama: Noel Coward was 20 when *I'll Leave It to You* was put on, Terence Rattigan 25 when *French Without Tears* opened. It is also true that the English Stage Company, which presented *Look Back in Anger* as the third production to play in repertoire during its opening season, was a gallant, high-minded attempt to restore some seriousness to the London stage and restore the writer to his rightful place of honour in the modern theatre; but even that was not so epoch-making – quite a number of groups had set themselves up with similar ambitions and ideals, and had rapidly sunk again without trace.

Yet somehow out of the combination of these elements

something new and exciting did emerge – largely because the time was ripe and everyone somehow conspired to think that it was new and exciting. And success bred success. First of all on the most elementary financial level: the gradually building financial success of *Look Back in Anger*, with its eventual harvest of film and publication sales, translation rights, etc., helped to keep the English Stage Company solvent and ready to produce more new plays by untried authors. The whole publicity hullabaloo about angry young men and all that also helped in a more general way to wake up the theatre-going public to the latest developments in British drama, and to arouse the interest of a whole new public. Exposure of a section of *Look Back in Anger* on television gave potential customers (even those who did not realize they were) a chance to sample the goods and see how they liked them, instead of depending on second-hand information and opinion culled from the critics. (This was the first time, but by no means the last, that television, supposed enemy of the theatre, intervened helpfully on the new dramatists' behalf.) And with this feeling abroad that something was up in the theatre, that there was excitement, reputation and even (magic thought!) money to be gained from the staging of new plays by unknown dramatists, things really got under way.

Ideas of this sort, naturally, are not self-sustaining. Particularly those which have to do with money. But the new dramatists came up with, as well as many plays that made more or less critical splash at the time and then sank without trace, a sufficient number of commercial successes, or at any rate plays which drew the public, to keep managers interested in them and them in business. The plays which fit under one or other heading in the ten years after *Look Back in Anger* might be tabulated as follows:

1956: *Look Back in Anger* (Osborne), *The Quare Fellow* (Behan).

1957: *Flowering Cherry* (Bolt), *The Entertainer* (Osborne).

1958: *The Hostage* (Behan), *A Taste of Honey* (Delaney), *Epitaph for George Dillon* (Osborne and Creighton), *Five Finger Exercise* (Shaffer).

1959: *The Long and the Short and the Tall* (Willis Hall), *One Way Pendulum* (Simpson), *Roots* (Wesker).

1960: *A Man for All Seasons* (Bolt), *The Wrong Side of the Park* (Mortimer), *The Caretaker* (Pinter), *Billy Liar* (Waterhouse and Hall), *Fing's Ain't Wot They Used T'be* (Frank Norman).

1961: *Rattle of a Simple Man* (Charles Dyer), *The Knack* (Jellicoe), *Luther* (Osborne), *The Kitchen* (Wesker), *The Devils* (Whiting).

1962: *Nil Carborundum* (Livings), *Two Stars for Comfort* (Mortimer), *The Collection* (Pinter), *Afore Night Come* (Rudkin), *The Private Ear* and *The Public Eye* (Shaffer), *Semi-Detached* (David Turner), *Chips With Everything* (Wesker).

1963: *Next Time I'll Sing to You* (Saunders), *Oh What a Lovely War* (Theatre Workshop).

1964: *Armstrong's Last Goodnight* (Arden), *Eh?* (Livings), *Entertaining Mr Sloane* (Orton), *Inadmissible Evidence* (Osborne), *The Royal Hunt of the Sun* (Shaffer).

1965: *The Killing of Sister George* (Marcus), *Ride a Cock Horse* (Mercer), *A Patriot for Me* (Osborne), *The Homecoming* (Pinter).

To which one might add a few more which had no noticeable success of any kind at the time but eventually came to be recognized as classics of recent British theatre, such as Pinter's *The Birthday Party* (1958), Arden's *Serjeant Musgrave's Dance* (1959), Charles Wood's *Cockade* (1963), and Edward Bond's *Saved* (1965).

All this, of course, helped to inspire confidence, or at any rate keep up hopes. And inevitably it contributed to a process which was bound to come into effect sooner or later: that by which inexorably the revolutionaries of one generation overthrow the establishment only to become themselves the establishment for the next. Nor in the arts is that necessarily discreditable; after all, new concepts do actually change the sensibilities of the public, so that the innovator does not have to turn into a reactionary once he achieves a position of power and responsibility; he can go on doing his own thing and developing along his own line, only now with public acceptance instead of mistrust or outright rejection.

This, happily, is what at any rate the leading figures of the New Drama have done. If anyone can be categorized as the theatrical establishment today, the established figures of almost unquestioned pre-eminence, it would be Osborne and Pinter. They are flanked by more inherently conservative figures such as Robert Bolt and Peter Shaffer, and are guaranteed, if not success (for who can ever be automatically guaranteed that?), at least a respectful hearing. So are many others, such as Wesker, Arden, Livings, Ann Jellicoe, whose status is less assured; if their work is rejected by the public, at least it is not rejected out of hand, from instant incomprehension. In that sense, the battle of the New Drama is won; it has become, almost without our noticing it, just drama, to be judged like any other. 'Experiment' in the theatre, deliberate innovation courting unpopularity and incomprehensibility, has for the most part moved to other areas than dramatic writing: to instant theatre, improvisation and the 'happening', to the work of self-consciously exploratory, innovating directors and designers. Though one or two of the very young, very new dramatists like Heathcote Williams and Howard Brenton seem out, on occasion, to prove exceptions to the rule, on the whole written drama, verbal drama, as opposed to improvised and non-verbal theatre, is almost by definition, however outlandish its style, taken to be Establishment, on the side of the squares.

But while this has been happening, if it has been happening (and there are many aggrieved dramatists who would violently disagree that it has), the external situation of the theatre has not remained unchanged. To begin with, the passage of ten or fifteen years brings about a natural, inevitable change in audiences: a generation dies, is scared off, or just drifts away into other activities; a new generation with new ideas and, even more influential, new preconceptions comes into the theatre. This has happened in the fifteen years since *Look Back in Anger* just as in any other fifteen years, only perhaps with a more immediately perceptible effect. It has been a by-product, I think, of another process which has affected not only theatregoing but filmgoing and reading as well: an increasing fragmentation and specialization among the public at large. What it comes down to, no doubt partly because of the constant spread of education, partly because of the ever-readier availability of rival attractions such as television, motorized travel and so on, is that now there is no such thing as *the* theatregoing, *the* cinemagoing, *the* reading public – the minority who do, consistently, as against the majority who don't, at all. There are instead an infinitude of smaller, more specialized, more choosy publics – almost to the extent that each play, each film, each book, has to find or create its own. And to the theatre, specifically, the broader divisions tend to be first of all by age, and then by education.

This means that there are theatres, plays which are patronized almost entirely by the middle-aged, who themselves divide into more and less educated groups, and others which are patronized almost entirely by the under-35s or the under-30s, with considerably fewer appreciable distinctions in educational background. The Royal Court's productions would generally come in this latter category (though certain of its plays, like in 1970 David Storey's *The Contractor* and Donald Howarth's *Three Months Gone*, prove able to appeal to other groups as well), and so do most of the productions in London's burgeoning theatrical fringe of off-West End lunch-time theatres like Ambiance and more or less experimental groups like the Open Space, which obviously recruit most of their audience from students and office-workers. Elsewhere the audience for basic farces and whodunnits, Anna Neagle vehicles, musicals and machine-tooled comedies imported from Broadway, remains defiantly middle-aged (in spirit if not always in years), with a heavy reliance on pre-sold coach parties from the Provinces. And there is always the third force, betwixt and between, of audiences, not too stick-in-the-mud but not too adventurous either, who patronize primarily the major subsidized companies, the National Theatre and the Royal Shakespeare Company.

In the Provinces, as in London, the last few years have seen a marked reversal in the consistent pattern of reducing audiences and closing theatres; instead, new theatres seem to be springing up all over the place. Of course, it depends what you mean by a theatre. Few of the new theatres conform to the old repertory pattern, still fewer fit into the virtually moribund touring circuit which used to ease productions on their way to or from the West End. Instead, a lot of them are linked with universities and educational establishments, and many more are improvised by groups and companies in whatever accommodation happens to be going. In London these informal and often peripatetic art centres have largely taken the place of the old theatre clubs, rendered obsolete by the final disappearance of the Lord Chamberlain's censorship in 1967 and some relaxations in the licensing laws which govern such places of entertainment. This sort of theatre suits the young, the eager, the ready-for-anything; its informality and even perhaps its frequent physical discomfort give it an atmosphere pleasingly unlike the old formality of the evening in Town, doing a show. If the theatre is still dying (and it seems to have been doing so for a very long time), it is only certain kinds of theatre, certain parts of the theatre, which faint and fail, just as their audiences faint and fail. But looking at the theatre in a wider context than that of the play in its setting and the theatregoing public in theirs, it does really rather look as though, taken by and large, it has seldom been healthier.

This is the situation which the first wave of the New Drama helped to make, and now stand to benefit from. But they can never quite adjust to the strangeness of it, and this marks them off in many ways from the second wave, those who have invaded the scene after the first battles of the New Drama have been fought and won (so much so that the newcomers are often not quite sure what they were all about), when the authority of the Lord Chamberlain was in rapid decline or abolished altogether, when the theatre was no longer one coherent thing (essentially West End-commercial), a citadel which had to be stormed, but might just be a basement somewhere where two or three (or two or three dozen) happen to be gathered together. It is the writers of this second wave, those who began to come to prominence towards the middle of the 1960s, that I have chosen to write about in this book – those who have established themselves since the first appearance of my earlier 'Guide to the New British Drama', *Anger and After*.[1]

They are not all young – or not, anyway, in comparison with the principal figures of the first wave. Peter Nichols and David Mercer, for instance, are older than Osborne, Pinter and Arden; John Hopkins is older than David Rudkin; and even Tom Stoppard, born in 1937, is still older than such an old stager as Shelagh Delaney, born in 1939. There are several younger, of course, such as Heathcote Williams (born 1941), Howard Brenton (born 1942), Christopher Hampton (born 1946), and David Hare, the infant of the outfit (born

---

[1] Direct quotations from the writers in the main text, when not otherwise credited, are from conversations with me.

1948), but they are in a minority. Nor do these writers fit neatly into groups, either according to their styles of writing – which range from the most conservative to the most advanced – or in their places of theatrical origin: gone are the days when a dramatist could be pinned down as a Royal Court or a Theatre Workshop writer, a television or a club-theatre man. They can be taken only one by one, as so many separate and individual phenomena – more or less in order of appearance.

Peter Nichols

Better late than never might well be the motto of Peter Nichols. At any rate, it had better be, since recognition did not come to him until he was pushing forty, with the production of his first stage play, *A Day in the Death of Joe Egg*, in 1967. At that point a lot of critics and theatregoers began asking excitedly where Peter Nichols had been all their lives, and were surprised, as is so often the case, to discover that he had been writing television plays for nearly ten years, and had written some fourteen of them, many in their time highly praised. But then, of course, the various media are still today so extraordinarily insulated from each other that probably no one could be blamed for forgetting, or never knowing in the first place. And as Nichols himself remarks, memories are so short in television: in a couple of weeks today's sensation will have faded almost completely from all our minds.

That is perhaps not entirely a disadvantage, either. Looking back today Peter Nichols feels, as do probably many other dramatists, that television was primarily a good place for him to learn his craft by trial and error. Some of his television plays he does not now think very highly of, and he confesses to regarding nearly all of them as a sort of second-class drama.

'I suppose it's largely the quite disproportionate prestige of the stage play, but I have always felt that on television I naturally work in a lighter register, don't go so deeply into my subjects, or don't in the first place pick subjects which require me to go really deeply into them. I admire playwrights like David Mercer who seem able to do their deepest and best work for television, but I think I should find it too disheartening, feeling that all my best efforts were going to vanish after just one airing, which quite possibly no critic would write about and would never get into print.'

Doubts or not, Peter Nichols's television plays are in fact by no means negligible. The play which achieved most fame and success at the time was *Ben Spray* (1961), a wayward and under it all perhaps slightly bitter comedy about a young ex-teacher on a night out. The hero is an inveterate but good-natured liar, whose feeling about communication with other people is basically that you can't. If he were anyone else he could perhaps manage; if he were a film stuntman, or a jazz musician, or even a Jew called Spratberg who kept coal in the bath, he might be able to get through. But being just Ben Spray, a lonely and difficult refugee from a language school who always makes a dead set at the most glamorous girls and always gets left with their plainer friends, he does not stand a chance. Whether a potential troubadour, as he suggests at one moment, or more suited to be a fool as someone else unkindly remarks, he is like a child and has the vulnerability of a child. He can be hurt, and during his night out he is several times touched a little too close to the quick; he is urged to outrage by unkind remarks about Negroes, he is used as an unwitting tool in a lovers' tiff, and his motives in comforting a little girl when she calls out at night are disastrously misunderstood. But like a child, he soon bounces back; he is an innocent but an indestructible innocent. The subject-matter was fashionable in television at the time: the shadow of Lucky Jim still lay heavy. But Peter Nichols's variation on the theme was sharp and personal: on the strength of this play in particular I popped him into the first edition of *Anger and After* the following year with some slightly sniffy but not, I think, entirely unfair comment about 'sprightly invention sometimes a little dampened by the exigencies of working-out'.

But *Ben Spray* and its sequel *Ben Again* (1962), which Nichols now regards as 'rather too determinedly lightweight', were even then by no means the best he could do. There were already signs of something more. In *The Big Boys* (1961) again there is a school in the background (Peter Nichols was once a teacher himself), but the story deals with what was to become a running theme in Nichols's work, the mutually destructive relations between children and adults – destructive in this case both to the little boy who takes poison before a school play and the master whose marriage is threatened by the revelation of his wife's infidelity. *The Reception* (1961) was on the surface a broad farce about a wedding that goes wrong. Things start going awry when the bride's former fiancé turns up uninvited with a present – a portrait of the bride in her underwear (so much more suggestive than a nude). 'He's being victimized,' shrills the groom's mother, a frosty, be-feathered matron in the best farcical tradition. Confusion reigns; rival factions locked in bedroom and bathroom turn on bride and groom. Unfortunately at this point the situation gets a bit out of hand, and not even the first excruciating moments of a party game involving a trio of fractious aunts could save it. But the character of the ex-fiancé, a disillusioned young man hardly angry any more, merely peevish in spite of his bland cynicism, did bring a touch of something sharper and more realistic, even at times uncomfortably so.

Two other television plays of this period suggested that Nichols had a distinctive talent, even if it was difficult to be sure exactly in which direction it would move. *Promenade* (1961) was a very slight, apparently aimless piece about a group of young people nearly all living on money from their parents and bolstering one another up in a warm sense of group security. But the slight plot allowed Nichols room for unusually rounded dramatization, and the eventual escape of two of the group from their lotus-eating existence took on real significance from our unusually close knowledge and understanding of what made them tick. *The Hooded Terror* (1963) was very different, and rather bizarre. Two young couples, one week-ending with the other, meet a hooded boxer in a local funfair and bring him back with them to give their babysitter a fright. But our expectations of this situation are neatly reversed: the apparently normal, agreeable couples prove to be torn apart by jealousy and prejudice, all of which is unleashed by the new situation the appearance of the boxer in their midst creates, while the boxer himself, for all his sinister aspect, turns out to be a true innocent, an honest and idealistic young man who feels an immense nostalgia for the settled family life he imagines he will find in his hosts' house. The idea, in particular, of the violence lying beneath the surface of ordinary, apparently conventional family life, is one which in various forms has recurred in a number of Nichols's plays, right up to and beyond *A Day in the Death of Joe Egg*.

Even more significant than these minor plays, though, is *The Continuity Man* (1963), which began life as a stage play written on an Arts Council bursary, but according to Nichols never worked out properly that way and so was eventually transformed into a television play. In this we have not only mutually destructive relations between the child and the adult, but – a particular Nichols refinement, this – we see them carrying on between parents and children until well after the children are themselves grown up and apparently independent. The principal characters are a modish young married couple who regard themselves as being decidedly a cut above the vulgar old father of one of them, and who yet prove to be still tied to their origins, shaped decisively by their original family situations. The play was too crowded for its television length (presumably because of some fairly drastic shortening in the rewriting), and the character of a glamorous film star, brought in to expose the emptiness of glamour as an ideal of life (she turns out to be an unhappy lesbian) seemed rather arbitrarily introduced. But the play had the core of a real idea, and passages at least which hit exactly that anguishing mixture of comedy and brutal reality which has become Peter Nichols's hallmark.

In some ways *The Continuity Man* is rather like a sketch for what I think is still Peter Nichols's best television play, *When the Wind Blows* (1965). I gather he likes it too, regarding it as the densest and in a way the most felt of these earlier works. It was, he says, the only one of his plays in any medium which pretty well wrote itself, perhaps because something very like it happened to him. Essentially it is the story of a tea-party which brings together an intellectual young couple and the husband's parents, a fairly solid, settled, ordinary-seeming couple, and develops into a sort of life-and-death battle over which pair will finally wreck the other. Unexpectedly, it is the young couple who survive, the middle-aged couple whose marriage breaks up as a result of the encounter. The effect is strange and haunting, and the play has resonances which continue in much of Nichols's later work, particularly *Joe Egg*, where Bri's mother is obviously the same character, basically, as the mother in *When the Wind Blows*, with her smothering, almost hypnotic affection and her continuing power to draw her grown-up son back towards childhood, and *Forget-Me-Not Lane*, which virtually recreates the central situation of *When the Wind Blows* in different terms.

Since the success of *Joe Egg* Nichols has actually had three major new television plays produced: it is perhaps a measure of the distressingly low standing even the best of television drama is accorded among critics that they received comparatively little notice. *The Gorge* (1965) is really a feature film made for television, showing the complex interactions of the generations during a family visit to Cheddar Gorge. The life of the family concerned is seen through the eyes of an intelligent and sensitive 16-year-old boy, and the picture is hardly flattering. Miles's parents and honorary aunt, together with a Canadian visitor, talk relentlessly in clichés, and such a thing as an idea never crosses their vacant minds: all their worries are bound up with respectability and the desire that everything shall be nice. The tone of the play is lackadaisical comedy, and the sympathy for once is fairly and squarely with the boy, in his attitude to his parents and in the embarrassing complications that his would-be idealistic relationship with a would-be earthy girl he meets on the picnic lead him into.

Daddy Kiss It Better (1969) looks at the same subject from the other end, that of the parents. It studies the break-up of a marriage in a kaleidoscopic pattern of flashbacks, and again the dominant theme is the mutually destructive relations of parents and children, in that the prime reason for the failure of the marriage seems to be the couple's children, who make companionship between man and wife difficult and arouse a sort of competitive jealousy in the husband. Here, as in all Nichols's other handlings of the theme, it is interesting to note that he has no truck whatever with fashionable interpretations of it in terms of generation-gap, non-communication between parents and children. His generations communicate, if anything, all too well, and the gap is negligible; indeed, central to his observation is a recognition that as we grow older we are quite likely actually to become our parents, to act out the same patterns of behaviour over and over again.

Hearts and Flowers (1970) begins like yet another piece about the destructive influence of children – a youngish married couple are in bed together, squabbling mildly because the magic has gone out of their love-life since the arrival of their two children, possibly soon to be joined by a third. But it rapidly goes off in a different direction; with the death of the husband's father we embark on an agonizing comedy in Nichols's best manner documenting in terrible and uproarious detail the progress of the funeral-cremation, with all the little social embarrassments and misunderstandings among a collection of socially and educationally varied relations and in-laws caught by Nichols with malicious – yet not merely malicious – precision. There is a bit more plot, concerning the relationship between the husband and his TV-celebrity brother (he didn't get on with father, the brother did, and, as it transpires, the brother was first in bed with his wife). But the funeral is the thing – it is the method of *The Reception*, applied to the materials of latterday Nichols, the suffering, the dying, the dead, depicted with full human sympathy, human dignity, which yet detracts nothing from the humour of their situation.

Nichols admits himself that the idea of the family as a sort of trap we cannot escape, which inevitably conditions us and forms us however we may subsequently try, consciously and unconsciously, to fight free, seems to be something of an obsession in his work. He even hopes to break away from it, regarding it as rather limiting. And perhaps he will. If *Joe Egg* is, among other things, his definitive examination of the family situation – which it can be precisely because it presents it in an extreme and obviously special form, which allows it to be all the more clearly dissected and analysed – *The National Health* suggests a move in a new direction, and there are indications all through his work to date that he can do other things if he wants to: the wayward comedy of *Ben Spray* suggests one way, the sophisticated comedy of manners and sexual infighting in the Bath sequence of his film script *Catch Us If You Can* (1966) suggests another: we would not, on previous experience, recognize in the bored upper-middle-class husband and wife who pick up the young hero and heroine on their way west and try, not very successfully, to use them as sexual playthings what one might call typical Nichols characters, and yet they are very vividly created – more so, certainly, than the rather colourless juveniles of the piece. And meanwhile he has made an obviously crucial breakthrough simply by writing two successful stage plays and proving decisively that his technical range is far wider, and more solidly founded, than anyone could have suspected from his television work alone.

The breakthrough came about first of all from the very practical reason that he conceived the idea of writing a play about the life of a family with a spastic child (a subject he could write about from first-hand experience), and realized that to write it truly to his own experience and observation, he would inevitably produce something which no television company would touch, so it had to be written as a stage play or not at all.

'You see, I had read practically everything anyone wrote on the subject, and it happened I was reading a novel on the same subject, *The Last of the Pleasure Gardens*, by Francis King. Now what struck me was that it, like everything else I had read, was very solemn about it all; you know, sort of hushed in the face of private grief. And that was not how I had experienced it at all. Nothing in my life has ever been really dignified: I always trap my finger in the door just when I am making a dramatic exit, and even the most serious moments of life always turn into grotesque comedy. That's why all my television plays are somehow or other comedies: I have used television as a sort of public diary into which I poured my observations as they occurred to me, and they always came up comic. The same here, except that no one, but no one, would countenance this subject in terms of comedy. So it had to be a stage play, and I'd just made enough money from writing *Catch Us If You Can* to take a year off from television and write it.'

It is hard to conceive, from the play which was so written, exactly how Nichols would have gone about writing it for television. Certainly, *A Day in the Death of Joe Egg* could hardly be more theatrical in its form and language. The whole of the first act is a duologue between Bri and Sheila, husband and wife, parents of Josephine, the spastic, known as Joe or sometimes Joe Egg. Well, strictly speaking, it is a three-cornered conversation, with the audience as silent partner.

The very opening of the play establishes the convention. Bri, who is a teacher, comes on and at once starts berating the audience, us, as his refractory class at school. The device is simple but effective: immediately we get used to being addressed from the stage, since this time we are playing a particular role in the play's world; hence, when husband or wife starts confiding in us directly from their cosy suburban living-room we are ready for it and accept without demur.

In any case, it is all an extension of the play-acting games which make up much of their life. The central fact of that life, of course, is Joe, a wordless, almost immobile presence centre-stage. And she is a fact it is difficult if not impossible to face head-on. So Bri and Sheila weave fantasies, joke round her if never making her a joke, act out little charades dramatizing facets of their situation. It all makes things more bearable. It also disguises, but does not altogether obliterate, the deeper troubles in the relationship between Bri and Sheila. For Joe, as we might expect from some knowledge of Nichols's earlier plays, is not only a personal tragedy both parents can – must – share. She is also a divisive influence. What each tells us, the audience, directly while the other's back is turned is a long tale of disagreement and dissatisfaction.

Sheila accuses Bri of being jealous of Joe, jealous of the attention which has to be lavished on her. He is in a sense a perennial child himself – the last person to be the father of someone who in a more concrete, literal sense is condemned to permanent childhood. Bri has a different slant on things. For him Sheila's wholehearted dedication to Joe, and to the idea of her improvement, perhaps even cure, is morbid. Joe is for her too, though in a different way, an excuse for contracting out of life; she may believe that in sacrificing everything for Joe she is being nobly self-sacrificing, but in fact it is finally the most selfish thing she could do, wrecking everything for her and Bri without even ensuring any corresponding advantage for Joe, who would almost certainly be better off professionally looked after in a home.

So much emerges in the first act, amid a constant dazzle of jokes, knockabout humour and the occasional tirade – the last being Sheila's in which she describes the day Joe first showed she wasn't a vegetable and gave Sheila the hope to continue, the faith in Joe's eventual improvement she needed to live by. In the second act we see the family in contact with outsiders: with another married couple, Freddie and Pam, who are or consider themselves slightly grander, and with Bri's mother, who 'just drops in' (we have already heard something about her in the first act – mainly through Sheila's blaming her upbringing for Bri's present childishness). The visitors represent the reaction of the ordinary, uninvolved outside world to Bri's and Sheila's predicament – which is basically one of remote sympathy, not wanting to know too much about it or come in too close contact, and probably having all sorts of 'principles' in the matter such as only the completely uninvolved can subscribe wholeheartedly to. Freddie sees his second purpose in being there for the evening (the first is to convince Bri, unnecessarily, that there is nothing between him and Sheila, as Bri affects to believe) as to 'Get them both to see sense about the poor kiddie'. His third purpose is 'to give poor Brian back an interest in life'.

It may be imagined that a social evening seen in such terms by one of the participants is likely to be an embarrassment for all concerned. And so it is. Freddie and Pam are in no doubt that whatever the right attitude to a family tragedy like Joe may be, Bri's and Sheila's apparently jocular, heartless approach is the wrong one. They understand the sound of desperation as a sick joke. Both Freddie and Pam are allowed to put their point of view directly to the audience too, and though they are slightly caricatured, almost as creatures of Bri's fantasy, they come often uncomfortably close to the mark in stating shamelessly what we may all at some time have half-thought and been ashamed properly to formulate. Some of what they say is even quite sensible – but in a situation where the 'sensible' is no longer enough. After all, in many ways the most 'sensible' solution would be the one Bri hints at more than once: euthanesia. And as the evening progresses it seems that may be exactly what Bri has in mind. His account of smothering Joe is just a joke, but has he really thrown away her anti-convulsant medicine, or given her an overdose? Certainly when he takes her out into the cold he hopes she will die, but even so he cannot quite go through with it, his plan to 'stop them saving her again'.

But of course they do: Bri in his best serio-comic vein describes the hospital emergency, the miracle-working doctor, the whole medical system being concentrated on prolonging Joe's pointless existence a little longer. At least one thing has emerged clearly from this latest crisis: that Bri's and Sheila's marriage is impossible. Joe's death might perhaps have saved it, but with Joe alive there is no room in Sheila's life for anything but her, and she feels the same should be true of Bri. As the curtain comes down Bri walks out, this time for good – and in the confident belief that Sheila will hardly notice his absence in the long term any more than she does at this moment.

It would seem that Nichols arrived at the play's very free and easy-seeming form by a process of trial and error. He explains:

'I'm no good at all at plotting. I write slowly, with certain fixed points and general ideas of how it will be in my mind, but I am dependent on finding my way as I write. In *Joe Egg* I knew from the start that it would be about an evening in the life of a couple with a spastic child, that it would start with Bri's teacher sketch (which was actually an independent sketch I had written years before), include an attempt to murder the child, and end with the husband's leaving. But beyond that I was hazy about the details. In the first version the two visitors were there from the start, in a rather Albee-ish situation, to be taunted and baited and used as a sounding-board by the host couple. But then it seemed to be a cumbersome and pointless device, so I took them out, let Bri and Sheila talk directly to the audience, and only brought them in in the second act, where they could be of positive use in the drama. (Curiously enough, no critic has ever commented on this delayed entrance as a piece of dramatic tactics.) Originally it was the man visitor who tried to kill the child, horrified by what he saw, and he succeeded. And Bri's mother was a late addition; some people think she shouldn't be there at all, don't see what she has to do with the play. But to me she's a sort of key – because she is what she is, Bri is what he is, and therefore his life is what it is.'

The play, having, for a wonder, got produced (first at the Glasgow Citizens' Theatre in 1967) went on of course to be a big critical success and a moderate commercial success – i.e. it ran for four months, which seems to be about the maximum for such a play in a West End theatre. It was then produced in New York, and adapted for a film. And indeed its success was deserved: no one could accuse it of being a television play which does not know its place; it manipulates the unique qualities of live theatre as an interchange between stage and audience with comsummate skill in the long monologues and direct addresses to the audience, and it does, to an extraordinary degree, carry audiences along with it, over the initial embarrassment of feeling that they are laughing *at* a spastic child to a wider, freer understanding that they are laughing not at people, but at the life situation which has caught them, as one way or another it catches us all.

Since *Joe Egg* Peter Nichols has written three television plays, the script of the film version of *Joe Egg*, and *The National Health*, which brought him to the stage of the National Theatre. *The National Health* has in common with *Joe Egg* a readiness to treat as a comedy what almost any other dramatist would treat, if at all, as the direst drama, and to make of it a comedy which is still entirely serious, and as far as possible from the conventional, flip gesture of 'black comedy'. This time the setting is a hospital, the dramatis personae are mostly the suffering and the dying. On one level, the play is a portrait of six patients in the male ward, with interventions by two more, a legless man noted for always keeping cheerful and a young motor-cyclist who is discharged at the beginning and comes back, reduced to a vegetable after another accident, at the end.

But mainly it is the six. Rees, the old doctor now himself dying who alternates between bouts of painful clarity and periods of obsession with the idea that a taxi is waiting for him if only he could get hold of his clothes. Ash, the depressive ex-schoolmaster with an ulcer who feels a sense of grievance because he had no success as a schoolmaster or a husband; and now even his step-son has no time for him. His protective instincts and frustrated interest in boys' welfare find an outlet first with Loach, a new arrival with amnesia (he claims), a prison record and a drink problem, plus a fund of barrack-room lawyer misinformation about hospitals, medicine and life, then, finally, with the motor-cyclist Kenny, whom he sees now as a perpetual little boy in need of protection. (Curiously, Ash appears here as a sort of amalgam of Sheila and Bri in *Joe Egg*, with Kenny playing Joe.) Then there is Foster, the accommodator to the system, usually deep in some radio programme, barricaded behind his earphones, who eventually, quite unexpectedly, drops dead. And Flagg, the prostate patient, whose whole life seems to be concentrated on urine bottles and bedpans. And Mackie, the terminal cancer patient, who asks for nothing better than to die peacefully, and is never allowed to – again, a theme from *Joe Egg* – since Mackie is, like Joe, a victim of the twisted pseudo-humanity of a system which moves heaven and earth to resuscitate someone whose life cannot be more than a vegetable existence or a constant battle with pain anyway.

The relations among these six, their reactions to their situation, to one another, to suffering and death, provide the main thread of the play. As in *Joe Egg*, the tone of their conversations is beautifully judged so that to a certain extent the play can be enjoyed on the level of *Carry On Nurse*, yet without our ever losing sight of the reality of the suffering, the fragility of the surface jokiness. As Philip Hope-Wallace put it, the play catches its audience 'between wind and water, half in tears and half slain with laughter'. But all this is still only half the play. Interspersed with the scenes in the ward are interludes on a simulated television screen, where unrolls the soap-opera of the play's subtitle, *Nurse Norton's Affair*.

In this, characters on the medical staff of the hospital reappear in glamorized fantasy, acting out a novelette about a black nurse's romance with a craggy Scottish doctor, the impediments put in their way by his crusty old father, also a doctor, and the high drama of Doctor Boyd's operation to save Neil, his son, with a kidney donated on the spot by the devoted Nurse Norton. All this is written with an uncannily exact feeling for the idiot conventions of dialogue and character in such series, and is riotously funny in its own right; but juxtaposed with the scenes in the ward it takes on a new significance. It represents, for one thing, an alternative form our fantasizing of medicine may take: patients are funny, doctors are romantic. It represents, also, the patients' fantasy picture of the medical staff, which they are able to accept despite its complete incompatibility with what they know from first-hand experience. And it could also be – though I do not think it is importantly so intended – a suggestion of the detached ruthlessness with which the medical staff approach the patients, not as people at all but as objects, at most, of theoretical interest: doctors and matron, for instance, never know any patient's name.

And linking these two sides of the play is the slightly mystifying character of Barnet, the orderly. Barnet is played throughout in a style of music-hall comedy, with addresses to the audience, outrageous innuendos and extravagant asides. In the ward he jollies the patients along, keeps things moving, plays up to their little fantasies, plays one off against another. In this respect he is probably a good thing, since at least he treats them more like human beings than anyone else on the staff. In the soap-opera interludes he acts as introducer and narrator, thus stage-managing the transitions from one form to the other as he stage-manages everything else. But there is another element in his character, which provides the real puzzle. Increasingly, as the play progresses, he takes on a demonic aspect, and eventually he turns quite nasty, especially with Loach, the alcoholic who is shakily resisting the idea of taking a cure: at the last we see Barnet pressing drink on him, and continuing to do so after he has (temporarily influenced by Ash) said no, until finally he says yes. The play leaves a slight feeling that Barnet is meant to represent something beyond himself which does not quite emerge. But even so, it is hard to find serious fault with the play, especially as produced at the National Theatre, or the character of Barnet as superbly played by Jim Dale (himself a recruit from 'Carry On' films).

As *Joe Egg* was originally thought of for television, so *The National Health* was originally drafted as a television play, in 1965. (Again, it has its roots in an experience of Nichols's own, when he was in hospital for a period and had all too much opportunity to study his subject at first hand.) The television version was turned down flat by every company, mainly on grounds of 'good taste' – even though one would have thought it evident that the play is, as well as being very funny, immensely compassionate. Perhaps its eventual success in Nichols's much elaborated stage version is a sign that we are now growing up sufficiently to take Peter Nichols as he comes, and even to take the world he pictures, our world, as that comes.

The enormous success of *Forget-Me-Not Lane*, both critical and popular, would seem to confirm this judgement. His third full-length piece for the stage, it looks very much like the play Peter Nichols has been in training to write for the last ten years. Not only does it bring together elements from at least five television plays, but it neatly resumes most of his leading themes – the 'genetic trap' which eventually turns us into our parents, especially in the ways we most hated and despised in them; the divisive effect of children on married life; the mechanics of parent–child and particularly father–son relationships – and offers, perhaps deliberately, a key to Nichols's work as a whole.

Obviously one cannot take it as simply autobiographical, though Nichols admits that there are strongly auto-biographical elements in it. But whether real or imaginary in detail, it does indicate very clearly how the various parts of Nichols's imaginative world fit together. It takes up again, as its starting-point (in time, if not in the theatre), the parent–child relationship shown in *The Gorge*, along with the abortive sexual encounter between an intelligent but painfully in-experienced boy and a much more earthy, knowing girl. This develops into the young–adult situation depicted in *The Continuity Man*, with the boy and his wife, who have now improved themselves with degrees, posh accents and all, coming back into the original family situation and being forced into a re-enactment of childhood patterns of behaviour.

This leads into a virtual rewrite of *When the Wind Blows*, where a cosy domestic gathering brings together a young couple and the husband's parents, and develops into a life-and-death struggle over which couple will finally succeed in destroying the other's marriage. But what was there played largely as drama is here presented in the context of comedy, and the parents' marriage, though severely bent, does not break altogether. This time it is the son's marriage which breaks up, in very much the circumstances of *Daddy Kiss It*

Better: husband's resentment of the demands children make on the wife's time and interest; wife's resentment at the way the husband forces her into the position of organizer, dominant partner, and then blames her for it. And at length the father dies, in just the way that the father died in *Hearts and Flowers*, and we see that with a few minor adjustments (the introduction of a brother to complicate the family and marital situation, in place of *Forget-Me-Not Lane*'s best friend) this is the same family exactly at a slightly later stage. (In fact, *Hearts and Flowers* was written in the midst of *Forget-Me-Not Lane*, as a footnote and a way of bringing the stage play into focus.)

From all this it may be gathered that there is, to say the least, an enormous amount of material in *Forget-Me-Not Lane* – a family saga covering three generations, no less. And the most astonishing thing about it is the way Nichols has managed to organize his material in such a way that one has no feeling whatever of overcrowding, and certainly no feeling of bittiness. Technically the play is an extraordinary achievement; instead of seeming, as it well might, like a jigsaw puzzle, it has the richness and unpredictable intricacy of veined marble. It is a very theatrical play, with a central character–narrator who uses to the full the possibilities of stepping in and out of the action, now becoming himself deeply involved, now stepping back sadly or ironically to comment.

The whole play, indeed, is built on a pattern of ironies, brilliantly manipulated. An effect will be meticulously built up, and then cheerfully undercut with some deflating comment or absurd juxtaposition. But the deflation is not merely destructive, a cancelling-out; instead it always brings us into something deeper, stranger, another layer in Nichols's complex, many-layered reality. This may be done by just one line, as when Frank, the hero–narrator, objects to being ticked off as 'sonny boy' by his father on the grounds that he is nearly forty and has three children of his own, and his wife at once tartly reminds him that at this stage he is nearly thirty and has only two children. Or it may be by a reflection that it is left to the audience to make, as when Frank, after recounting to us one of his most embarrassing experiences, when his puritanical father interrupted a blue comic's act at a local variety show, concludes that this put him off audience participation for life, and we automatically observe that this is a funny thing for Nichols to say (in so far, of course, as it is Nichols rather than his character who says it) when so much of his technique depends precisely upon the degree to which he gets his audiences to participate.

But more than by these overt devices, however ingeniously used, the play works its ironies on us by subtleties of structure. I can think of few plays in the contemporary British theatre where the dramatic syntax is so functional. The form seems to be free, taking us backwards and forwards in time more or less at random. But if we stop and consider for a moment, each episode proves to be placed where it is, in relation to its surroundings, with the utmost nicety. The placing of the scene in the theatre, for example, right out of its chronological context, at the end of the play, gives it the effect of summing up, in microcosm, the whole involved relationship of father and son, and the characteristic they most obviously have in common, a strange and guilt-ridden sexuality. In the same way the exact order of Frank's reminiscences throws light on his character from half a dozen different directions, so that we find ourselves sympathising with him in an obvious, naïve way (seeing things through his eyes, we are put in his position), then gradually detaching ourselves as we see him less and less sympathetically – particularly from his wife's point of view – and come to apply to him and his family just what he has been saying about his parents and their relationship: that it is all a matter of interpretation, of where you stand at any given moment.

That may be how the play works, but it does not give much indication of what it is working for. As well as being a devastatingly acute dissection of the family situation (any family situation), it is, for a start, a riotously funny theatrical entertainment. Of course it is not 'just' funny; as we know already from *A Day in the Death of Joe Egg* and *The National Health*, Nichols is most serious when he is most funny, he has a unique gift of finding the laughter in pain without diminishing its painfulness. If you think about his plays, you don't know whether to laugh or to cry; but in the theatre, for the moment at least, you laugh. And in *Forget-Me-Not Lane* the laughter comes loud and long. The character of the father is quintessentially the sort of parent who is fine in someone else's family but agonising in one's own, especially amid the manifold built-in embarrassments of adolescence. We laugh, as an outsider would, at his catch-phrases (beautifully graded, incidentally, to indicate the passage of time and shifts of relationship) and his little jokes, but at the same time we cringe along with his son at the sheer social horror of it all.

And above and beyond all that, the play is a hymn to the Forties, to the generations whose monument was the Festival Hall. Ah, the romance of the runaway barrage balloon, the big bands with the big beat, pin-ups of Betty Grable, slap-and-tickle in the shelters, the surrealistic splendour of casual bomb damage. Yet even here there is a built-in irony. When Frank extols austerity (it sounds so much better than affluence) we see that he has been crippled by the times as much as by his individual family circumstances; adolescent in a masochist's paradise, he carries the psychological scars of guilt and repression into his own forties. If he ends by turning into his father (his lecture on his own now-teenage son on noise and motor-bikes is a masterly transposition of his father's thought-patterns into his own generation's liberal vocabulary) it is not only the genetic trap which has done this to him; it is the times he has lived through, and his understandable but misplaced nostalgia for them.

From almost every point of view *Forget-Me-Not Lane* looks like a summary of Nichols's work to date, gathering together its various threads and presenting them to us in a satisfactorily rounded whole with even more dazzling skill than *A Day in the Death of Joe Egg* or *The National Health*. And yet it is a real play; it gives completely the illusion (if it is an illusion) of organic growth; it resolutely shows us everything, tells us nothing. That is why we understand so much from it. And indeed the success of Nichols's campaign to broaden our dramatic responses probably derives first and foremost from the fact that he never set out to mount such a campaign, never had any intention except to write single plays mirroring an aspect of the world as he sees it. 'Robert Bolt once told me that each time he has an idea, then he sets to work to embody it in a play,' says Nichols. 'I don't think I have any ideas, any statement I want to make. I just seem to keep on writing plays.'

David Mercer

It is seldom, even today, that a headline in the *Radio Times* has some sensational news to impart. But many readers in February 1970 must have been pulled up short by ' "This", says David Mercer, "is my swan-song to politics".' 'This' was his latest television play, *The Cellar and the Almond Tree*, or rather the trilogy of which it is the middle section: and the intelligence would be news indeed, seeing that of all our new playwrights Mercer is the one who has most consistently worried at the political theme in his works. Indeed, it is hardly too much to say that he is the only one who seems to have felt, as a dramatist, more than an occasional, dutiful interest in politics, in man as a political animal, and in the dramatic possibilities of political life and political action as a vital part of his characters' everyday existence.

The news, as it happens, is not quite so clear-cut as the headline-writer made out. In the body of the piece Mercer is quoted as saying that the trilogy is 'partly my swan-song to conscious politics in drama' and in a television interview on *Line-Up* after the play he amplified this statement as representing a feeling that he had, not that politics as such was a dead subject for him, but that it was becoming part of a wider and more inclusive world-view which made it less and less possible for him to confine his characters within an explicitly political framework. That is rather different, and indeed is something we could have seen for ourselves right away in his very earliest plays, the trilogy called *The Generations*. There the progression was clear enough. The first play, *Where the Difference Begins* (1961), was easily the simplest and, superficially, the most realistic he has ever written; it was a straightforward piece of social documentation about the growing-away of two sons from their working-class father because of the changes made in them by education and by their inevitable graduation (or decline, if you like) into the middle classes. The second play in the group, *A Climate of Fear* (1962), moved out into a direct confrontation with the most burning political issue of the time, nuclear disarmament. But already in the third, *The Birth of a Private Man* (1963), the clear political issues are complicated and confused by cross-currents of individual personality, by the impossibility of confining complex, contradictory human beings with simple formulas, political, psychological or any other sort.

The progression in these three plays is technical as well as in the subject-matter. *Where the Difference Begins* is awkward with the hangover of kitchen-sink realism: it goes about establishing its situation – deathbed of working-class mother precipitates the arrival of two sons, Richard, with a divorce pending and a pregnant girl-friend, Edgar, the priggish one with an irritable wife and a planned family, and sets them off right away arguing under the benign, understanding eye of their railwayman father Wilf – with some clanking of convention, getting people on and off stage and telling us things we need to know by having characters tell one another things they know perfectly well already. The issues are talked out, sometimes rather stodgily and didactically, rather than dramatized. But all the same the play has a certain slogging power and integrity. Obviously of the two sons Richard is the more attractive, but he as much as Edgar has been irrevocably cut off from their parents, especially the father, by education and training: they have both, whether they want it or no, become members of the middle classes, and cannot make their way back to a certain working-class strength and innocence (as Mercer then sees it, personified in the character of Wilf). That is finally where the difference begins, and the difference, once there, cannot be glossed over.

By comparison the form of *A Climate of Fear* is much freer –
already Mercer is indulging in that free-ranging verbal
elaboration, restoring eloquence to the small screen, which
was to become his hallmark as a television dramatist. It is not
literally a sequel to *Where the Difference Begins*, but it takes as
its starting-point the relationship between Edgar and his
wife Margaret in the first play, complex, edgy, the old,
conventional, unquestioning devotion shattered and nothing
very clear to be put in its place. In *A Climate of Fear* Edgar and
Margaret Crowther become Leonard and Frieda Waring –
rather older, with teenage children of their own (though the
period is the same as in *Where the Difference Begins*). He is a
nuclear scientist; they are both middle-class liberal intel-
lectuals, and the tensions of their situation, their attempts,
often muddled and self-contradictory, to remain humanly
involved in the world about them and its issues create the
'climate of fear' in which they and everyone else in the play
live. In the writing Mercer takes off from the basic four-
square realism of *Where the Difference Begins*; the style is more
ornate and even at times poetic, and the dialogue is clearly a
distillation of thought and feeling rather than a straightforward record of, more or less, what such people would
really say in such situations.

The drama of the play is really Frieda's. She has let herself
hide away in a private world of generalized liberal emotions,
but now she is being forced to take decisions, to come to grips
with awkward realities, largely by the activities of her
children Colin and, especially, Frances. It is Frances who
uncovers all the details of Frieda's abortive relationship with
Peter Driffield, a radical university lecturer, and with
unthinking cruelty throws them all in her mother's face.
Leonard is a hollow man, unable to see things clearly as they
are or react otherwise than in a set pattern, but Frieda can
still feel, and so can, if only very painfully, be redeemed. The
high point of the play, in fact, is her long monologue in bed,

in the course of which she digs deeper and deeper into her own most secret, unavowed fears and confusions, to come out in the end wiser, sadder, and more ready truly to live, to keep herself open to experience, even the hardest to live with.

Other themes recur from *Where the Difference Begins*, notably the legendary working-class heroes of simpler and perhaps therefore happier days, represented by Leonard's dead father Surry (Wilf in the first play) and Peter Driffield's father Tom, who while out of his depth in the complexities of the modern world retains even as an anachronism the primitive stature of Socialism's heroic days. And there is also a lot in the play which looks forward to *The Birth of a Private Man*: the characters of Colin, rebel and enthusiastic CND supporter, and Frances, working her way painfully towards intellectual and emotional maturity; but also the part played by Peter, the rebel without a cause, the radical mistrusted by every faction whose notions, so clear and effective in the realm of abstract ideas, prevent him from taking any simple decision to act in everyday life. The various, related predicaments of these three characters suggest the need to work out a new individual solution to the problem of life, or as many individual solutions as there are individuals to require them. If Jimmy Porter is right, that there are no big causes left, this does not absolve us from the necessity of finding a reason for living, a way by which we can respectfully live with ourselves. If there are no ready-made answers in mass movements, we must find our own answers; the conditioned political animal must give way to the private man.

In *The Birth of a Private Man* we see a way that this may come about. The private man who is slowly, painfully born is Colin Waring. The play begins with the death of Tom Driffield, a sort of symbolic farewell to the heroic generation. Immediately afterwards Colin announces that he is going to withdraw from politics into private life, disillusioned not so much with his ideals as with the ability of men ever to live up to them. He is going to marry his girl-friend, have a family:

'All she wants is babies and peace. Not peace movement; peace. Peace is a room with a child on the floor. It would be strange, wouldn't it? To stop agitating. Turn your back on everything. Watch your wife grow pregnant, take a job, furnish a flat, keep your head well down. In a world you believe the public men will destroy.'

It is one way of becoming a private man; by contracting out. But it is not a way Colin can follow (unlike his father, who did so without even being conscious of making a choice); his attempt to do so is only one symptom of his progressive disintegration, driven mad by the horror of the world around him, in which he sees destruction as 'the most incorrigible force in the human personality'.

The play follows out his disintegration. He travels, first round Britain, then to France, and finally to Germany, to Berlin, getting madder and madder, more and more obsessed with his black vision of a world of horror made by man in his own image. In the end the only thing for Colin is suicide, a sort of ritual self-immolation on the Berlin wall, accusing both sides and belonging to neither, nothing really but himself, a poor, bare, forked animal, a private man. But that is not all there is in the play. To balance Colin there is a new character, Jurek, Frances's Polish fiancé. His view of life, formed by sufferings in a concentration camp, is not much different from Colin's. But unlike Colin he believes that giving in, contracting out, is too easy a solution. More painful, but absolutely necessary, is to go on fighting, with one's eyes wide open to the tragedy of life. Jurek, faced with a choice, chooses to live. In the process, he too has been reborn as a private man, but a man whose privacy does not cut him off from the world around. Instead he preserves within himself the humane values he believes in and hopes in due time to contribute them to the new society he looks forward to and in his own way works to formulate.

The contrast between Colin and Jurek is fundamental to the play's structure. But since this is the culmination of a trilogy, in which we as well as the author may be assumed to have become interested in the fate of a number of characters, our curiosity is gratified – though always in a way which reinforces the main theme. Frieda has now taken a decision and left Leonard; her relationship with Peter, irritating to Frances because of its untidiness, continues, but she is making her own life working in the children's ward of a hospital. She too has the courage to face life and become a private person. Peter is, as he must be, unchanged and unchangeable. Frances too is unchanged: the passage of time has not matured her, softened her, brought her to any closer understanding of life's complexities. Perhaps nothing can; perhaps her immaturity is a permanent defect of character. But if anything can, Jurek, marrying him and living in an actual Communist society in Warsaw may do it. Certainly Jurek sees the necessity of opening her eyes, breaking her of a certain naïve, inhuman dogmatism if their marriage is to work, and at the end of the play they are left, maybe, on the threshold of a new mutual awareness; possibly, just possibly, Frances may escape from the toils of her simple-minded, dogmatic approach to life, and become in her turn a private person.

Indeed, looking back now, it is possible to see the whole body of Mercer's work as depicting in various ways the birth-pangs of a private man. His characters are all involved, one way or another, in the battle to assert their individual, unique natures within, or if necessary outside, the framework of normal everyday life, of social, political or psychological categories. To say that all are involved in this struggle does not necessarily mean that all of them consciously engage in it, and it certainly does not mean that they all win out in the end. Some seek comfort in anonymity, uniformity, some contrive to contract out of the struggle, some are shattered by it and destroyed. But behind the action of all Mercer's plays is a consciousness of individuality as something which is constantly under attack, and which has to be fought for with all one's strength if it is to be preserved.

This continuing theme in Mercer's work gives unity and direction to the expression of his various personal preoccupations. The principal preoccupations are political and psychological – or are usually categorized as such. But it seems to me that the attempts of various commentators to define Mercer's work in terms of a 'polarity' between politics and psychology, Marx and Freud, are finally quite beside the point, in that there is no appreciable tension between the two concepts, or two ways of looking at things, in the plays themselves. Instead, both are seen as essentially the same thing, or rather, one might say, both are interchangeable metaphors for the real subject: the relationship between the individual and the institution. Thus in the group of plays that Mercer wrote after *The Generations* there are several about people who are mad or are going mad. *A Suitable Case for Treatment* (1962), *For Tea on Sunday* (1963) and *In Two Minds* (1967), for example, all deal with aspects of the same subject, which one might capsulate, not unfairly, as social alienation expressed in terms of psychological alienation. So does Mercer's first stage play, *The Governor's Lady* (originally written for radio in 1960), in which the governor gradually turns into an ape, and his first full-length stage play *Ride a Cock Horse* (1965), in which the hero gradually regresses into total infantilism, thus contracting out of the fight for survival as a functioning individual.

At the time *Ride a Cock Horse* was about to be produced, Mercer explained his position in this group of plays about insanity thus:

'It seems to me that the logic of events has carried us beyond the phase where it was possible to give oneself simply and whole-heartedly to clear-cut causes like nuclear disarmament. The realities of the moment are the *détente*, the affluent society, the virtual disappearance of the big, clear issues upon which socialism fed between the wars. Perhaps there are no big causes left, but it is too late to complain about it, and pointless anyway; what we have to do now is to discover how we can live in a world without big causes. The only possible revolution is the individual revolution; any expression of individuality, however small, is a revolutionary gesture. Anything, in fact, that helps us to escape from categories. I deeply distrust categories: sane, insane, criminal, law-abiding and so on. Psychologists, sociologists, politicians all deal in categories, and very constricting categories at that; it is curious that still, more than half-way through the twentieth century, we should still be psychologically dominated by two arch-exponents of nineteenth-century rationalism, Freud and Marx. Now the "lunatic" fascinated me, I think, because he is the man who, almost by definition, escapes from categories. I don't think I am sentimental about lunacy; I don't regard the lunatic as some sort of divine fool whose experiences necessarily have greater validity than those of the sane. But on the other hand I feel that the dividing line is much too arbitrarily drawn, largely to reassure us that sanity is better and that the experiences of the insane, if they do not fit in with our preconceptions, must be quite without validity. I don't really believe this; these things happen, these experiences are undergone, and it must mean something . . . I think we have to redefine sanity by looking occasionally through madmen's eyes, or we are depriving ourselves of whole areas of experience, we are, as it were, voluntarily chopping off psychic limbs so that we can fit into categories which are largely artificial anyway.'

The first play to express something of this complex of ideas, taking up from where the Colin sequences of *The Birth of a Private Man* left off, was *A Suitable Case for Treatment* (later filmed, none too faithfully, as *Morgan*). This was actually seen on television before the third part of *The Generations*, thus slightly obscuring Mercer's line of development (as did, even more, the belated appearance of a play he wrote immediately after the first draft of *Where the Difference Begins*, *The Buried Man*, eventually done on television as *A Way of Living* (1963), which dealt in a similar, solidly realistic fashion with the division between a young man from a fishing family who intends to continue fishing and a girl from a mining family who is about to go on from grammar school to Newcastle University). *A Suitable Case for Treatment* is characterized in its published version as a 'comedy' – and so it is, but a comedy with a very serious point. Morgan Delt, like Colin, cannot come to terms with life as he sees it. Instead, he withdraws into a world of knockabout fantasy. He is a writer who doesn't write; divorced by his wife, on whom he has lived for years, he still insists on scattering her flat with booby-traps and spying on her affair with his agent; both his wife and his mother have taken on the status of symbolic fantasies in his mind, which is otherwise peopled with, most agreeably, apes, a species with which Morgan feels a nostalgic affinity ('If I'd been planted in the womb of an orang-outang, none of this would ever have happened'). Finally – for this is after all a comedy – he decides to pull himself at least partly together and go and live with Jean, a telephonist who loves him. Why? Well, 'She's alive', and choosing her is a gesture in the direction of life, one way out of an unending regression. (The ending of the film, also scripted by Mercer, was perhaps significantly much nearer to despair, even though much of what went before had been played all too uncomplicatedly for easy laughs.)

An even clearer expression of Mercer's identification of the social and the psychological theme in his work is his next play, *For Tea on Sunday*, also classified in its published form as a 'TV comedy'. What happens in it is that a group of girls sharing a flat have the habit of bringing in their men friends for Sunday tea – a nice, comfortable, social occasion until one

Sunday the young man one of them brings in happens to be mad, and systematically wrecks the whole easy, recognizable pattern until at the climax he actually takes an axe to the furniture, and perhaps, unless he is stopped, to the other people present. The level on which this action is conducted may be that of social comedy, but the implications are deeper and more disturbing. At bottom the young man's madness emerges as an expression of, or an image for, a feeling that the times are out of joint, that indeed perhaps the whole of human history has been leading us confidently along quite the wrong track. This is not, as Mercer himself insists, a sentimentalization of the mad as a sort of repository of truth which the rest of us, the 'sane', have lost. Rather going mad is seen as a last, no doubt ineffectual but for some people inescapable, rearguard action in the battle to preserve a degree of personal integrity, of unclassifiable individuality, in a world where our natures are for the most part deformed by the need to conform.

Whereas Nicholas in *For Tea on Sunday* is seen only at the end of his tether, and the drama (not to mention the comedy) is derived mainly from the reaction of other 'normal' people to him and his extreme, physical way of contracting out, in *Ride a Cock Horse* we observe the progressive stages of Peter's regression into total infantilism. Peter might almost be Richard from *Where the Difference Begins*, a few years further on. He is a successful writer of working-class origin, much like his wife (they both have socialist heroes in their immediate family background), but cut off from his roots by the difference of education, success, middle-class acceptance, he is growing increasingly unable to cope with life, to meet it face to face. He seeks evasions of one sort or another, in drink, in fantasy, in relationships with two women besides his wife. And gradually what begins as comedy becomes no laughing matter, as he is pulled apart by his own internal conflicts, the impossibility of living with his political convictions and of living without them, until he regresses to a state of complete infantilism, curled up on the bed in a foetal position from which, apparently, only the last-minute appearance of his father (a wordless image of working-class solidity in a cloth cap) can recall him.

Is the play serious or funny? Like most of Mercer's later work, it is both. Though the central situation is deadly serious, it is dealt with, as in *A Suitable Case for Treatment* and *For Tea on Sunday*, with a lot of wild and wayward humour, particularly in the sexual skirmishing, which one would hardly have imagined from *The Generations* to be within Mercer's range at all. Though another early play might have warned us: his one-acter *The Governor's Lady*, written immediately after *Where the Difference Begins* but never performed until the Royal Shakespeare Company took it up in 1965. It is an extravagant fantasy about a colonial governor and his wife in which the governor gradually becomes, as his wife sees it, more and more 'animal' until he literally turns into a gorilla and is shot by his lady. She confides to her diary that she believes he is going mad, but it is probable that if anyone is going mad it is she, driven by her own frustrations. But that is no doubt to rationalize too far an elusive, polyvalent dramatic image. The oddity of the play, at the stage of Mercer's development in which it was written, is that it is so non-social, except by remote implication, and thus fitted in so well with what he was writing five years later, in which his principal interest seemed to be in the area where the civilized façade breaks down.

Mercer himself commented on this curious dichotomy at the time of *The Governor's Lady*'s stage production:

'I wrote it immediately after *Where the Difference Begins* and then went on with the rest of the trilogy. But at the same time another side of myself entirely was finding expression in a group of short stories which were comic, fantastic, extravagant, and quite different from the me expressed in my plays. I wondered then how these two halves could co-exist independently of each other, and whether they would ever come together. I think in my latest plays they have: I now see drama not as a theatre of ideas in which questions can be posed and conclusions reached, but as a sort of ritual, synthesizing disparate and contradictory elements, accepting that personalities are fragmented, that truths are infinitely ambiguous, and yet binding together all these centripetal elements of the universe so that they are held suspended, mysteriously bound by the very tensions that always threaten to tear them apart. I suppose all I am saying really is the old cliché that art should synthesize, but at least this idea has helped me to get over my earlier fumblings and worries. I used to be a worried writer, always looking over my shoulder and wondering whether what I wrote would be acceptable to my friends or the party, whether people would love me any more, whether they would understand me beyond the possibility of doubt. Now I find that of course people misunderstand me from time to time, and it sometimes irritates me; I was irritated, for instance, when a critic accused me in *The Governor's Lady* of making a naïve equation between racialism and sexual frustration, and I wanted to write and explain to him that the play is really about one character, the governor being only a projection of his Lady's less avowable suppressed desires and instincts. A few years ago I would probably have been busy altering a line here, a phrase there, to make sure that such a misunderstanding could not happen again. Now I simply accept that there may be ambiguities I did not consciously intend and leave it at that. I think I have learnt at last to stand by what I do instead of just doing what I think I can stand by.'

Though it is certainly not true to say that David Mercer is one of those writers whose private life and background need to be known before his work can be fully understood and enjoyed, some information may be helpful. He was born in 1928 in the North – like his central characters in *Where the Difference Begins* and his later stage play *After Haggerty* – the son of an engine-driver. His subsequent career sounds, as he

has remarked, in some respects like a parody of the ex-
working-class intellectual, mark one. He did not get into a
grammar school, left school at fourteen, did various odd jobs,
including a spell in the Merchant Navy, before arriving at
Durham University. Then he had ambitions to be a painter,
went to Paris, but decided that he would never make a first-
rate painter, and turned his attention to novel-writing
instead. Before long he decided that his novels were no good
either, and then suffered a lengthy nervous breakdown, and
an even longer course of psychoanalysis. When he wrote his
first play (which was *Where the Difference Begins*) he was a
supply teacher; since it was accepted for production he has
been a professional writer.

The career gives a clue to a number of points in his plays.
The political development from old-fashioned liberal socialism to Marxism to his present position of being, as he puts it,
'a Communist without a party'. The important early contact
with psychiatry, and first-hand experience of mental illness.
The inevitable interconnection of the two involvements in
his own life reflecting on his plays, and his plays, equally,
reflecting on his own conscious thought. For Mercer regards
himself very much as an unconscious writer, quite unaware
of what impels him to write or what he is putting into his
writing until the writing is actually there before him. 'Once I
have written something I do feel a compulsion to examine it
and try to find out why I wrote it, what I was getting at. But
at the time I write, I am completely in the dark about what
I'm doing or where I'm going.' No doubt this is the reason
why changes of position, or at least of emphasis, are appreciable in his plays some time before he is himself altogether
conscious of them.

In particular, this applies to the most recent developments
in his writing, which are clearly signalled first, I think, in *And
Did Those Feet?* (1965), a very strange television play about
twin brothers, one very fat and the other very thin, who are

the only children of an ageing lord. Unfortunately they are illegitimate, and their father, though constantly remarrying, is quite unable to produce a legitimate heir. Consequently he hates Timothy and Bernard, especially as they seem to live in a world of their own where his hate can hardly touch them: they have virtually given up ordinary commerce with other human beings (even their official girl-friends play a puzzlingly peripheral role in their lives) and joined the animals. For a while, they work in a zoo, but finally they cannot bear it any more and let the animals out. Later they settle in a deserted swimming-pool with swings and a lot of rubber animals which they intend gradually to replace with real animals, and in the end, after their father has been shot by their mother (who lives most of her life as, literally, a bird in a gilded cage) they set off, disregarding the vast fortune they have inherited, for the Amazonian jungle, where no one can interfere.

All this is written in a rich, eloquent style far removed from Mercer's early, naturalistic work. It is full of incidental symbols, some of them almost naïvely direct: Lord Fountain cannot have legitimate children because the class he represents is doomed; the artist character is represented as an Establishment figure to show that art is no longer an effective way of opting out of society, and so on. I do not find this objectionable though, as many critics have done, because these images are not at the centre of the play, but simply one quite telling way of dealing with lay figures who could not be characterized in much detail anyway. The central characters, Bernard and Timothy, are far more complex, defying any such simple formulation, and on them the play securely rests. As they progressively contract out of the everyday world about them, their purpose seems to be to get back closer and closer to a state of existence in which there is no appreciable gap between man and the animals, or indeed between animals and inanimate objects. To put it another way (an obviously loaded way), they hanker for a sort of prelapsarian state, before man had been isolated in the universe by Original Sin. (The connection with Morgan's passion for apes in *A Suitable Case for Treatment*, or the Governor's unfortunate transformation in *The Governor's Lady* can hardly be altogether coincidental.) And significantly, though he disclaims any particular religious affiliation, words like 'redemption' crop up increasingly in Mercer's formulations of his ideas. Redemption from what? Well, to begin with, I suppose, redemption from human institutions. To suggestions by critics that in his recent work he has become increasingly pessimistic, in that he seems less able to see a panacea for mankind's problems either in politics or in psychology, Mercer replies that his present position is neither optimistic nor pessimistic, but, he believes, a more realistic appreciation of things as they are.

Which is to say, that 'institutions are necessary, and at the same time are necessarily doomed'. We hanker after some sort of disciplined framework for our lives. But at the same time, every attempt to provide such an order, though necessary to our continued functioning, is bound, like Frankenstein's monster, to take on an independent life of its own which has nothing to do with its original purpose, which is even, sooner or later, inimical to its original purpose. This is true of all Churches, of all political parties, of all psychological theories, of every pattern devised by the human mind.

'It may be that if we are all in the same boat, we have been in the wrong bloody boat ever since Plato. What we need is a new boat, or no boat at all. And by now it is probably too late to roll back the whole history of Western civilization, to get back to sources and start again. But it seems to me that this is precisely what a lot of people, individually or collectively, long to do at this point in time.'

Most of Mercer's later plays respond to interpretation in these terms. *Belcher's Luck* (1966), Mercer's second full-length stage play, is about maverick vitality which escapes from all neat, dry, intellectual formulations, but is finally defeated by them – the institution winning out over the individual. *Flint* (1970), deals with a variation on this theme, this time in the shape of an unmanageable old cleric, a shameless lecher who asserts that he has been agnostic ever since ordination, and yet is felt to be, in his crude animal vitality, of more value than the institution he nominally belongs to and is in constant conflict with. (No, says Mercer, he is not having a go at the Churches: the play could equally well have as its background a political party or Unilever.) And three of the other recent plays, *The Parachute* (1968), *The Cellar and the Almond Tree* and *After Haggerty*, are all directly concerned with memory, which represents in each case a retreat into a past which, whether happy or unhappy, was at least manageable, comprehensible, showing a pattern which gave some sort of shape to life. The subject is obviously ambiguous. The looking-back can be interpreted either as a bad thing – an irresponsible escape from present reality, a block which prevents one from living satisfactorily in the present – or it can be seen as good (or as humanly inevitable), in that it perhaps reflects the constant attempt to return to sources, to find out where one started to go wrong in order to start again.

But, as we might expect, none of these plays, nor any of the others he has written during these years, is all that simple. Even when the basic theme is fairly clear, the details of its working out, and even the author's apparent attitude towards them, vary enormously from play to play. Two of the later television plays, for example, *Let's Murder Vivaldi* (1968) and *In Two Minds*, seem to be offshoots of *Ride a Cock Horse*. *Let's Murder Vivaldi* is occupied entirely with sexual infighting: there are two couples, Ben and Julie, who aren't married, and

Gerald and Monica, who are. Neither arrangement seems on the face of it very satisfactory: Ben and Julie are constantly quarrelling and threatening to break up, but never do; Gerald and Monica talk distantly of divorce, and lacerate each other with cruel wit. And despite an attempted affair between Gerald and Julie, nothing changes, because nothing can change. Facing reality or rationalization of that which cannot be cured so must be endured? Who can say – but Mercer writes it with such glittering wit and precision that it does not seem to matter very much. Where *Let's Murder Vivaldi* plays variations on the barbed marital comedy of *Ride a Cock Horse*, *In Two Minds* takes up the mental breakdown theme again – for the last time so far in Mercer's work. This time the victim is a young woman, Kate, a schizophrenic, and the play pictures, at times in an almost documentary fashion, her attempts to deal with the people round her, with life, and to live up to the contradictory and often unreal demands people make on her. Her insecurity is partly a means of escape, but then she has, as we see, much more to escape from than any of the doctors dealing with her seem to imagine – to them there is 'apparently no detectable relationship between her various symptoms and her environment'. But, guided by Mercer, we are in a position to know better.

These two plays in their different ways look backwards in Mercer's career. *Belcher's Luck*, on the other hand, starts from where *And Did Those Feet?* left off. It is a fable, or a parable; it is certainly above all an extravagant, even fantastic tragi-comedy which cheerfully shuffles aside any sort of literal trust in politics or concern for abstract formulations. Belcher is a great bursting fertility-figure, the servant of a doddering landowner and moving spirit of the estate, which he has ruled almost as his own for forty years, scattering it with illegitimate children, keeping it fruitful, and presuming that the death of old Sir Gerald will make little difference to his position. He has particular grounds for supposing so, in that his illegitimate son Victor has been educated up by Sir Gerald to be his heir. But everything changes with the arrival of Sir Gerald's niece, Helen. She is as cold-blooded as Victor, but in a different way; whereas he represents the negatively debilitating effects of education and upper-class culture, she is savagely mercenary and materialistic. She and Victor make common cause, but first she urges Belcher to finish the old man off. Once he has done so, he is summarily dismissed, while the bloodless younger generation take over. He is given one last gesture, though: we have learned earlier that the only creature he really loves is a mare, and before leaving the estate he shoots the mare down. The play is very much all-over-the-place, but bursting with eccentric, unpredictable life, and shows another side of Mercer from his overtly political pieces, an anarchic humourist who neatly slips out of any formal category we might be tempted to press him into on the strength of his most familiar television plays and *Ride a Cock Horse*.

Belcher's Luck is not necessarily frivolous, but it is not serious in the rather schematic way that these others are serious. Like all Mercer's more recent plays, it carefully avoids any too clear-cut conclusions, any rigid formulations of its subject-matter: whatever Mercer is doing in them he is not preaching. In many ways the other play of his it most resembles is *Flint*. Flint himself, the reprobate parson hero, is a close relative of Belcher's, though somewhat more urban and genteel. He has been an agnostic ever since he took orders, has bedded every possible girl (and quite a few boys too) and continues, even in old age, to do so. He is clearly, like Belcher, some sort of earth-father, a Laurentian embodiment of animal vitality in whose presence most others dwindle into nonentity. Not altogether his wife Esmé, who has retired to a wheelchair after their wedding-night and so left the field symbolically clear for him, nor her sister Victoria, later on his mistress but now in her turn discarded (she finally knifes

Esmé, for no very clear reason). But they remain quite peripheral (too peripheral, indeed) to the main business of the play, which is showing off Flint in relation (and usually in collision) with the Church, with the respectable, with the world at large; with practically everyone in fact except his last conquest and little winter love Dixie, a pregnant Irish girl discovered in his church suffering from an overdose of pills. Along the way some shrewd points are made at the expense of the Anglican Church (a rather easy target, to be sure) especially in the character of the worldly, amused bishop who has to deal with Flint, and there is a certain amount of cosy, familial fun made of the Communists too. In the end Flint is suspected of setting fire to his church, which he denies, runs away with Dixie, and eventually sets fire to himself while rushing on his motor-cycle to get help for her as the labour pains start. It is a funny, strange, consistently inventive play, and, like *Belcher's Luck* I think, not meant as much more than an entertainment in the Graham Greene sense of the term. On which level it works admirably, even if its lack of 'important' content seems to give serious people pause.

Nobody will accuse Mercer's latest sequence of four television plays of lacking 'serious content'. Actually the first of them, *The Parachute*, seems originally to have been conceived as a single, free-standing work – an historical piece hopping backwards and forwards in time between 1940 and the present anguish of Werner von Reger, a young Luftwaffe pilot, and the past, in which we see him torn between his father and mother, an elegant, intelligent, formally hostile couple who might be a German aristocratic equivalent of Gerald and Monica in *Let's Murder Vivaldi*. Werner's father tells him: 'Your mother sees you as a living rebuke to me; I see you as a vehicle for my detestation of her; and you see yourself in a good position to exploit the pair of us' – or, of course, to be crushed in the conflict between them. But, as usual in Mercer's writing, it is the relationship with the father which is particularly important, which is, indeed, psychologically crippling; admiring him, after a fashion, Werner stands aside from life, from the commitment even of a decisive relationship with his would-be revolutionary cousin Anna. And in the end, perhaps intentionally, perhaps not – even he does not know for sure – he cripples himself physically as well as psychologically by opening his parachute too late in a test jump. With his mother out of her mind and the sky full of Russian parachutes, he is left waiting passively to see what, if anything, will happen next.

There is no direct connection between *The Parachute* and the first play of Mercer's latest television trilogy, *On the Eve of Publication* (1969). This seems to me, on the whole, one of Mercer's less successful pieces. Though it has the advantage of being unmistakably a part of Mercer's own private world, with all the political and post-political preoccupations intact, and he uses its complicated structure of flashes backwards and forwards in time with great confidence, Mercer does, I feel, rather overestimate the degree of interest and sympathy we are likely to experience faced with the glum and boozy self-interrogations of his hero Robert Kelvin, a successful Marxist writer (cf. Peter in *Ride a Cock Horse*) who worries because he is really part of the Capitalist world he denounces in principle and is contributing nothing to the cause of revolution. The second play of the trilogy, *The Cellar and the Almond Tree*, is a great improvement. It consists largely of a meeting between a Communist party official, Volubin, whom we have already heard spoken of in *On the Eve of Publication* as a friend of Kelvin's, and an old Countess, the mother from *The Parachute*. During their meeting Volubin's mind goes back constantly to his most intense experience, probably his last real experience, when he was tortured and his girl-friend went to Moscow, never to return; the Countess as we saw at the end of *The Parachute* is more than a little dotty, and cannot accept that a Communist revolution has taken place, so her mind correspondingly reverts to gracious days before the war, when everything was in its right, predictable place. The occasion of their elusive encounter is a minor matter, of who should actually hold the keys to the wine cellar of the countess's ancestral home, now owned by the new Communist state; but the image it presents of two characters, each in a different way locked in the past, prisoners of memory (very much as Robert Kelvin is in the first play, come to that) remains intensely vivid. The third play, *Emma's Time* (1970), takes up the story of Kelvin's young girl-friend, Emma, from the first play, and reintroduces us to Kelvin, who has also popped up very incidentally in *The Cellar and the Almond Tree*. It starts after Kelvin's death, and then proceeds to move forwards and backwards, reconstructing the course of Emma's relationship with Kelvin in flashback and showing her attempts to adjust to the fact of his death in the present. These include a brief encounter (not very successful) with a Hungarian film-maker documenting Kelvin's life, meetings with Kelvin's mother and his childhood friend Charlie Bourne, and finally a meeting with Volubin, an emigré who wants Emma to help him write his 'unwritten journal' – a prospect which seems about to woo her back to life again.

In the whole of the trilogy (or tetralogy if you care to see it that way) Mercer is, as usual, following out his own pre-occupations, redefining his own part in terms of his most recently achieved attitudes. His whole œuvre, in fact, can be seen as a series of attempts at self-definition, each having its essential truth to the particular moment of Mercer's life at which it was written, but none written in the real hope of achieving the ultimate, unquestionable truth beyond the truths. *After Haggerty*, his latest-written play (apart from a short monologue for a white Rhodesian racialist, *White Poem*, written for a Sharpesville commemoration in 1970), is another attempt in the same direction. It intercuts the memories of two characters, Bernard Link, a dramatic critic who has given up activity, political and emotional, for a seat at the ringside, watching others fight it out, and the strident American girl who pushes her way into his household looking for the vanished Haggerty, an unseen presence who sends, or has sent on his behalf, telegrams of instruction at various times during the course of the play, and finally announces his own death on the freedom trail somewhere in Africa.

Again the subject is withdrawal – withdrawal into the past which may or may not involve a revaluation of the past. Both Bernard and the girl have withdrawn, permanently or in her case perhaps temporarily, from the battle of life. So, even earlier, has the third leading character, Bernard's awful old father. Essentially he is the same character as the father in *Where the Difference Begins*, only now with nearly all the heroic aura of working-class struggle taken from him. Sure, he still sees himself as a revolutionary figure, but with the passing years he has ossified into an embodiment of reaction, or closed-mindedness. The difference between the two versions of the same character (both, coincidentally, played by the same actor, Leslie Sands) over ten years or so tells us a lot about Mercer's own development during this time, his own reassessment of his past and of his political heritage. Without any particular inside knowledge one could guess that Mercer's relationship with his own father must have been crucial in his development, as it is in that of so many of his heroes, however like or unlike Mercer they may be. *After Haggerty*, returning in a sense to Mercer's very beginning as a dramatist in *Where the Difference Begins*, seems to bring his work full circle; though from what has gone before we can hardly doubt that it will prove also a jumping-off point for further investigations into his own nature, the nature of all of us, and our relationship with the world about us.

Mercer himself says now that he feels he will become

increasingly preoccupied as he grows older with 'the sense of the past being irrevocable'. This may be true; and yet already in these most recent plays Mercer partly gives himself the lie. The past may be irrevocable and Volubin and the Countess in *The Cellar and the Almond Tree* are effectively trapped by and in their own pasts. But on the other hand the past may exist only in the present: we constantly re-create our past to serve our present needs. If Mercer's characters cannot do this, or in *After Haggerty* are able to do it only partially, intermittently, Mercer himself seems able to do better than they. In his ability to plunge down into the past only to surface again with material to his present purposes, to remould the past so that it can be of some use here and now, lies the best guarantee that his work will continue to develop, and continue to excite, well into the future.

Charles Wood

One of the most spectacular jobs done by our newer dramatists has been to reclaim for the theatre, or to chart for the first time in some cases, areas of life and experience which have been neglected or ignored by previous generations of theatrical writers. The working classes in general were little considered in serious British drama, and hardly ever treated without some clear elements of patronage, between the Manchester school and Arnold Wesker (*Love on the Dole* notwithstanding). Particular localities have come to our attention in the theatre largely through the work of particular dramatists: Liverpool through Alun Owen, the Vale of Evesham through David Rudkin and Peter Terson (though how about Tyneside, Lincolnshire, Bristol, Cornwall?). David Turner has revivified the Jonsonian comedy of humours, Alan Ayckbourn the boulevard farce, John Arden the ballad opera – each reviewing and transforming the genre to his chosen ends. And Charles Wood, of course, has given us an unmistakable, unforgettable picture of the modern army – or for that matter of the military idea and the military man at any period since the dawn of time.

Needless to say, that is not all he has done. If the army is his central theme, it is not by any means his only theme, and he must sometimes get tired of being stuffed into a pigeonhole marked 'army expert', and thereby conveniently written out of detailed critical consideration. All the same, right through from his first produced play (or at least the first I can remember), *Traitor in a Steel Helmet*, all the way to his latest major work, *'H', or Monologues at Front of Burning Cities*, the army, the military theme has been of constant recurrence in virtually everything he has written, whether for stage, television or film. From his work, then, one might deduce that, of all his experiences, being a regular soldier from the age of eighteen to twenty-three (1950–5) has made the deepest impression on him. Next in importance, perhaps, is that of being born into the theatre, the son of actors touring the country in the most humble theatrical circumstances, and later working as a scenic designer and stage manager: obviously a lot of this has rubbed off on *Fill the Stage with Happy Hours*. And third, I suppose, comes the experience of actually being a writer, which comes up in the fictionalized autobiography of his television play *A Bit of a Holiday*, and its sequel *A Bit of Family Feeling*.

If the subject of military life has been consistent in Wood's work, the way it is treated has varied considerably. As might be expected, there has been a considerable stylistic evolution. His first two plays, *Traitor in a Tin Helmet* and *Prisoner and Escort*, were both written for television (though only the first was produced there at the time – 1961), and both in a pretty straightforward, naturalistic style. *Traitor in a Tin Helmet* is a *drame à thèse* – perhaps too evidently so. A couple of soldiers on a military exercise, a sergeant and a trooper, are injured when they wreck their car in a training area, and are rescued by a rather nutty down-and-out who has secretly taken up residence in a ruined farmhouse right in the middle. The sergeant is decent but limited, a soldier who lives by the book, while the trooper is more gentle and sympathetic, and makes some real attempt to understand their weird host. The latter has plans to live on alone, supporting himself in back-to-nature conditions, growing his own food and interfering with no one. But he wears a tin helmet he has found, and finally he is killed, accidentally, in the course of the exercise. The helmet seems, therefore, to represent a continuing, if unacknowledged, military presence in his life, and the lesson of the outcome is apparently that no one can just contract out:

the fantasy of an army exercise represents an omnipresent and inescapable reality.

Prisoner and Escort, at least in the version which was first presented on stage as part of Wood's triple bill *Cockade* in 1963, shows a considerable advance in subtlety and precision. Wood says that its origin was directly autobiographical ('this was real-life me taking a deserter back to Shepton Mallet'), and the cast of the play consists of the prisoner being escorted on a train, his two escorts and a girl who gets involved with them along the way. The escorts are respectively a leering, juvenile sadist and a parrot-like idiot trying constantly to live up to his company and surroundings in both knowingness and brutality. The prisoner is a born victim, edgy, difficult and ineffectual, too muddled to explain his actions even to himself, let alone anybody else. His most spectacular crime, it seems, though by no means his only one, has been to urinate on the boots of a German officer during some combined Anglo-German parade. Why? He insists he is not anti-German. But possibly it was some kind of obscure revolt against the whole business of war, the idea of constantly, senselessly reshuffling, for ever lining up with yesterday's enemies to fight yesterday's allies in ghastly, pointless repetition. However, this is something the play leaves us merely to guess at: Jupp (the name is the same as the trooper's in *Traitor in a Tin Helmet*, and the two characters are perhaps meant to be the same man) is quite unable to tell us, and in any case is no uncomplicated liberal hero – when he finds out, for instance, that the girl who has been pleasant to him has a coloured lover, his reaction is one of powerful, unthinking revulsion.

In other words, though we might be tempted to see *Prisoner and Escort* as a straightforward piece of tape-recorder naturalism, a slice of army life, it soon becomes clear that the impression is only skin deep. The detailed and to most audiences picturesquely exotic rendering of army speech proves on inspection to be a meticulously worked out, highly patterned fantasia on military themes which permits all sorts of things to emerge without ever directly stating them or forcing us to some simple, clearcut judgement. Even the eminently dislikable Corporal Blake, the man in charge, is presented straight, as a phenomenon, neither heroic nor villainous, but just there. Compared with some of Wood's later work, of course, the play is still quite easy and approachable: the army talk, with its mixture of special vocabulary, rhyming slang and bits and pieces of dialect from here, there and everywhere, is fascinating because it is novel on stage (and such is Wood's concern for topicality here that some of his slang was noticeably updated even in the short time between stage production and eventual television production – the stage's HOSKINSON: Been for a slash en I? BLAKE: Long enough for a Barclay's en you? becomes 'Been for a sprinkle, en I?' 'Long enough for a Jodrell') but it remains unobtrusive enough to be accepted merely as local colour, rather than requiring us, as Wood's later plays do, to enter wholeheartedly into a strange world of which the speech is only one, relatively superficial element.

More of what Wood was shortly to be at emerged in the third section of *Cockade, Spare*. The action of this takes place, or appears to take place, in some sort of military museum, with the tattered regimental colours fluttering from the roof, three highly irreverent soldiers cleaning up down below and grumbling about a fourth who isn't there. A sergeant-major comes along to inspect them, they get him telling tales about the heroic past of the regiment, and it gradually develops into a war game which is not really a game at all. Then the action in effect starts all over again, with the tales this time about a different campaign, a different collection of heroes. Little by little we get the idea that the museum is not really a museum at all, but a dramatic metaphor for the army as a whole, for military life with its mixture of garbled, rather cynically observed tradition, its slacking and skiving, and above all its terrible boredom, from which the only relief is war itself. Within the play we seem to see two turns of a slowly revolving wheel: things change little by little, some get killed to be replaced by others almost identical, old soldiers grow older and fade away, but above and beyond the details, military life, the army itself, flows on unchanging and unstoppable.

But all this, though reasonable and I think true, is merely interpretation. Wood works throughout by indirection, speaking in metaphors which could be interpreted a number of ways. He does not construct, or attempt to construct, a reasoned intellectual argument; instead he builds a mysterious and compelling theatrical experience, made of rhythms and lights and colour and noise and silence. It is perhaps not surprising, then, that even those who agree completely on the quality of the experience can disagree quite sharply on what they think it means. In particular, Wood's attitude to the army has proved a stumbling-block. In an age when militarism in any shape or form is a dirty concept for most critics, and the army, if not merely ridiculous, is a suspect organization to your average liberal-minded London playgoer, it was inevitable that the first conclusion most people jumped to was that Wood must be necessarily anti-army, and be attacking the army in what he wrote. But there is little or no unambiguous evidence to this effect in the plays themselves; on the contrary, what mainly emerges is a loving fascination with the army as a way of life, which is examined with the ethnologist's dedicated exactitude and refusal to pass moral judgement. It is entirely in keeping with the effect of his dramatic writings that Wood should insist he is anti-war but pro-army; and even war, in *Spare* as elsewhere, is shown as terrible and absurd, but perhaps after all an absurd necessity, a condition of life as well as a condition of death.

What Wood presents, in fact, is an anatomy of military life, and of war. He is not simply, propagandistly pro or anti;

he is eager to find out, and eager for us to join in the search for, what makes it all tick. Some of his lesser plays provide pungent comments on this. *John Thomas*, for instance, the middle section of *Cockade*, is a little parable about playing with fire, the timid bourgeois's dreams of power and uniformed glamour which make him a pushover, when it comes to the point, for anyone with even a little real power, a little real willingness to use force. So, we see a timid schoolmaster dream of acting out his secret power-fantasies in boots and a fascist uniform, but he crumples immediately when a policeman-figure promptly takes them from him and dons them himself. The television play *The Drill Pig* (1964) and the one-act stage play *Don't Make Me Laugh* (included in the RSC's *Expedition Two* programme in 1965) come at the question from the other side, both more light-heartedly exploring the no-man's-land between military and civilian behaviour. In *The Drill Pig* we are shown two contrasting soldiers in their army context and in their civilian (or semi-civilian) private lives; and the conclusion is suggested that the awkward newcomer, with his awful wife and in-laws, will shape up in time as just as dedicated an exponent of military spit and polish as the 'drill pig' sergeant who now has to deal with him. In *Don't Make Me Laugh* the comedy involves a sergeant, his wife who gives dancing lessons, and their life in married quarters with an awkward lodger whose presence tips the balance between military and civilian attitudes to life now this way, now that.

But Wood's definitive picture of the army as an institution and a way of life comes in his two major plays, *Dingo* and *'H'*, both of them written for the National Theatre, though owing to an intervention by the Lord Chamberlain, only the second was actually produced there. These two plays form a group in his work with a couple of his screenplays, that (adapted from the novel by Patrick Ryan) for Richard Lester's *How I Won the War*, and the original (though history-based) *Charge of the Light Brigade* for Tony Richardson. But in each case the film seems like a sketch of the play: the ruthless destruction and recurrence of characters in *How I Won the War*, the ghoulish, joyless humour too savage to associate with the flip gesture of conventional 'black' comedy, finds its ultimate statement in *Dingo*, Wood's agonizing dissection of modern warfare; *The Charge of the Light Brigade*'s largely realistic rehearsal of historic follies, military and human, is capped by the fantastic and unrelenting stage spectacle he has woven in '*H*' from closely comparable material (one of the principal characters in '*H*''s Indian Mutiny, indeed, proclaims himself to have fought in the Crimea first).

Neither *Dingo* nor '*H*' lends itself very well to simple (let alone brief) verbal paraphrase; both, like *Spare*, are shattering stage experiences which largely dispense with plot, reduce characterization as we usually understand it to a minimum, allowing characters to shift, fuse, change places, die and come back to life with dreamlike freedom and unpredictability, and depend very importantly for their effect on hitting us below the belt, Theatre of Cruelty fashion, by-passing the intellect and making straight for the guts. *Dingo* takes place partly in the North African desert, partly in a prisoner-of-war camp, and is a sort of unending parade of clichés from films, plays and fiction about the war, fighting and being a POW. Except, of course, that every cliché is turned inside out. Wood's soldiers are doggedly consistent only in their determination not to be heroic, not to swallow any of the bull dispensed by top brass, not to sentimentalize themselves, one another or their situation. Suffering here does not ennoble; it embitters and then, very rapidly, deadens, kills off the ability to feel, at any level, even the most basic ('I haven't had a good toss-off in months', complains one character early on; 'I've got nothing to inspire me'). Montgomery, Churchill, Rommel – all the heroic figureheads are savaged, and in their place is put nothing but a bloody-minded determination to hang on, somehow, emotionally cauterized in a world which has gone mad.

The very opening is characteristic. Dingo and Mogg, the two principal characters – Dingo a regular, Mogg a conscript very insistent on his civilian status – talk aimlessly about their troubles in the heat and the desert until interrupted by the arrival of Tanky. He has just escaped from a burning tank in which his mate Chalky is still trapped, screaming. Their reactions to this situation are hardly heroic or compassionate:

> TANKY. Shut up, Chalky – belt up, you bastard.
> DINGO. That's it. Get it out of your system – you'll feel better.
> MOGG. Burn – you bastard.
> TANKY. I've got to get him out.
> DINGO. He owe you money?
> MOGG. He'll be all right when his brain goes.

Thereafter Dingo and Mogg direct Tanky and a navigating officer into a minefield, or what they believe to be one, though unfortunately there are no explosions, and then exchange bets on the screams of the potential victims. Then they have a long conversation exchanging erotic fantasies and pouring scorn on each other's, until at length they both masturbate. While they are doing so a burlesque scene at the front of the stage introduces us to Rommel and a perfect stereotype stiff-upper-lip British officer, exchanging civilities. When Dingo and Mogg come back they meet Tanky again; he has retrieved the charred corpse of Chalky from the tank and now dandles it on his knee like a ventriloquist's dummy. The rest of the act counterpoints the conversation of Dingo, Mogg and Tanky (whom they eventually persuade to throw away Chalky by convincing him that it is actually the body of a German) with a rowdy comedian's show, full of low humour and moral uplift, and the irrelevant histrionics of a group of brainless hero-figures, spouting all the right idealistic sentiments to the accompaniment of Elgar.

In the second act the scene shifts to a POW camp, where Tanky and Dingo circle each other endlessly in a small boxing-ring, talking seemingly at random about escaping, why they don't bother to try, and the best way to contract out of the whole bloody business and survive. Meanwhile, on the beaches of Normandy the Comic is discovered spouting patriotic sentences, seated on the recumbent form of Mogg. When Mogg makes his presence felt he is instantly promoted sergeant-major. Before he can do anything heroic he is captured and finds himself in the same camp as Dingo and Tanky, whom, in his newly fledged authority, which makes him automatically a 'hero', he starts to berate as collabora-tors because they are not escaping. In the cause of morale he kicks Tanky's head to a pulp, getting very excited in the process. With the arrival of the Comic and three 'girls' in long blonde wigs the whole proceedings turn into a show again, with the slogging battle between Dingo and the new NCO Mogg continuing in the intervals of burlesque Oscar Wilde and an elaborate escape which finally leaves only Dingo and Mogg in the camp.

The third act shows us the camp again, now smartened beyond belief by the enthusiastic efforts of Mogg. Mogg, Dingo and Willie, the lovable German guard, are waiting for the arrival of the victorious Allied Armies, which persistently refuse to appear; there is intermittent wailing on the wind, and Mogg is subject to fits of anger. The victorious Allied Armies, as it happens, are more concerned with the post-war political carve-up, but when they eventually do arrive at the camp they are suitably moved at the spectacle it presents – 'life on the parade ground of Caterham'. Tanky is proclaimed a hero, having died; the only trouble is that he will go on about having been killed by a British NCO. The Comic is again master of ceremonies, running the victory distribution of honours like a television quiz show as the various characters we have met before – nearly all now dead – come up with their tales of daring exploits and require rewarding. Only Dingo stays stubbornly alive, stubbornly realistic: all he wants is to go home to his wife.

'That's what I blame the bastard for more than anything, chopping off, more like wearing away, rubbing down my compassion to not a thing, it is nothing. Alamein, Alamein, Alamein. What was this wailing, it was the wailing of my wife – it was the wailing of myself, it was the wailing of all I have seen die and it was nothing.

'It is such a pity this war was not fought for them . . . I might have kept my compassion, I might not have felt guilty, which I don't, because everybody will say it was fought for them.

'It was not. It was fought for all the usual reasons.'

At the last the Comic becomes Churchill, and Dingo asks 'Am I a fool, are we fools that comedians are set to lead us?', and the curtain comes down on Tanky moaning insistently 'He killed me. He killed me. He killed me.'

No doubt it was the considerable violence of the language in *Dingo*, its nicely calculated and relentlessly insistent obscenity, which scared off the Lord Chamberlain. But it is only a part of Wood's complex and nightmarish vision. *'H', or Monologues at Front of Burning Cities*, reinforces the point in a vast and complicated historical pageant play which follows Havelock's notorious, superficially victorious and in human terms disastrous march across India to the relief of Lucknow (which in the event only made matters worse, in that the relieving force was itself promptly besieged in the Residency with those it had come to save, so many more mouths to feed). Havelock himself was a favourite Victorian hero, and Wood does not satirize him as he did the World War II heroes in *Dingo*: he just makes terrifyingly clear the absolute divide, beyond any imaginative leap, between the command and the men, between heroic Christian ideals, however sincerely held to, and the bloodthirsty day-to-day realities. And the final judgement is not only that someone had blundered (as a matter of fact, no one had done much else), but that it is all pointless: as Surgeon Sooter, the only character able partially to bridge the gap between ideals and realities, observes, 'This dull bludgeoning we do has no lesson to teach anyone, except he should not do it do he wish to keep himself alive a time, and I wonder at the wisdom of that.'

The play starts with a prologue on the subject of mysterious Indian customs, as encountered by the British army, and particularly on the infamous cartridges allegedly greased with a mixture of pig and cow fat, so as to offend equally any Muslim or Hindu who was required to bite off the end. Ensign Mullet, dutifully explaining the whole business to the troops, is cut down by the Havildar and the Indian Mutiny duly begins. What follows is a kaleidoscope forming, scattering and re-forming groups of characters. There is Captain Jones Parry, a not unreasonable, not inhuman, not dishonourable man who should, the author observes in his introduction, be the real subject of the play. There is his stiff, religious wife, fated to get raped by mutineers (but only half-caste mutineers; rape would be against the religion of the rest) and like it. There is Surgeon Sooter, drunk but efficient, the only relatively dispassionate realist of the group. There is Colonel Neill, the inhuman self-styled 'Scourge of God', ready to commit the most extreme barbarities strictly by the book. There is Havelock himself, idealist and gentleman, if hardly a practical man of the world, regarding the whole campaign as a sort of religious crusade, and his son Harry, treated too often as a child, fit only to be seen and not heard. And later there is Sir James Outram, sent to take command over Havelock's head, who deliberately stands down for him but remains an ambiguous presence, sowing the seeds of uncertainty in the command.

We follow these, and many more, through the whole course

of the disastrous campaign, as Havelock and his forces fight their way to Lucknow to relieve the Residency there, by way of Cawnpore, where the spectacle of mutineer brutality inspires a matching wave of brutality among the British soldiery. Havelock finally dies a hero (though hardly a hero's death), without ever understanding his soldiers or what the war was all about or where he went wrong. All the bitterness and bloodshed is wasted (or nearly all of it). The epilogue is delivered by Captain Jones Parry, now father of a suspiciously dark child by his well-raped wife, in Dilkusha Park, eleven years after the prologue; he presents to his son the conventional heroic picture of it all, but it is punctured by Mrs Jones Parry's parting shot, the last line of the play, addressed to her child: 'Timothy, this is where your father was shot and died in agony.'

The play, unlike *Dingo*, is full of verbal splendours: great rhetorical outbursts of flaming eloquence as well as Wood's astounding command of intricately styled colloquialism. But what is most shattering about '*H*' is its mastery of sheer physical stagecraft. Sometimes, it is true, the play seems to call for a fantastically equipped ideal theatre of the mind, and the National Theatre, with its stylized toy-theatre setting (introducing 'a note of archness', according to Wood), did not always manage to live up to the text's exacting requirements. But the whole conception of the play, its bold use of colours and tableaux, and especially the masterly use it makes of an all-purpose front-cloth to shape and define the physical action, is triumphantly of the theatre, theatrical. The limitations of the theatre become positive advantages, allowing the dramatist to take all sorts of short cuts, to escape from exposition and literal scene-painting. One cannot for a moment imagine this text working anywhere but in a theatre, and that, in this day and age, is an extraordinary enough achievement.

It may be doubted whether even with *Dingo* and '*H*' Wood

has worked the army right out of his system. But certainly of late he has shown himself increasingly willing to look elsewhere for his subject-matter. He has written many film scripts, ranging from the Beatles' second film, *Help!*, to the English dialogue (a masterpiece of vituperative invention, if nothing else) for Fellini's *Satyricon*, and from Skolimowski's *Adventures of Gerard* to John Schlesinger's forthcoming *Hadrian VII*. Not all of them are, I suppose, equally personally involving for him, though the sometimes pretty strained fantasy farce of *Help!* seems to represent the same kind of ambition as the even more strained fantasy farce of *Meals on Wheels* (1965), by general consent Wood's weakest stage play.

It is about an elderly young man in his late thirties who devotes most of his life to running around after his old father (94, but doesn't look a day over 50) and his elder half-brother, bringing them meals on wheels prepared the other side of London by a dotty sister and trundled in on a little hand-trolley, and collecting money with the laudable purpose of having the two of them frozen by a new American process to remain in a state of suspended animation until someone invents a cure for old age. Near the beginning of the play John P has some new ideas put into his head by a nude painting in the local art gallery, and under the mixed-motivated guidance of the gallery attendant, a dirty-minded puritan with sadistic tendencies, begins to look for a wife, or a girl, or something. The obvious choice would seem to be his sister, as she herself remarks, after her eleventh imaginary pregnancy (a balloon clasped to her stomach) has been abruptly terminated by a passer-by, but there is a vague feeling abroad somewhere that this is not quite possible. In the end, though, everything works out all right, I think, because while the gallery attendant is making free with a lush armless model (full-sized) which John P has run up in his spare time in the religious-statuary studio where he works (to aid his concentration when sublimation becomes too much),

John P himself runs off with a life-sized statue of the Virgin Mary which is accepted by his family without demur as a suitable mate for him.

The result, perhaps meant to be a riotous, surrealistic knockabout comedy, is arid and mostly unfunny. A lot of the dialogue is clearly humorous in intention, and some of it is even humorous in effect. In particular the dirty stories with which it is the attendant's wont to prove his points about life and love and the ways of the world are still often good for a laugh. But that is not the whole play by any means. Much of it is taken up with considerable expanses of semi- or pseudo-army slang which, though no doubt managed with some virtuosity, are almost impossible for any but the highly trained ear to follow and, being also endlessly repetitious, prove pretty tedious to most of the audience. A suspicion persists that perhaps the play means to say something about puritanism, suppressed violence and the nature of British society, but if so it sadly fails to communicate. Presumably Wood himself agrees on reflection; certainly he has since remarked that the play was written for production in Bristol, with close reference to a local Bristol scandal, and lost all relevance or even comprehensibility when put on in London after Bristol Council had refused to allow it. Anyway, the play was never published in its original form, and when it reappeared in Liverpool in 1970 as part of a triple bill called *Welfare* it was considerably shortened and revised as a one-acter.

Far better in every way have been Wood's semi-autobiographical pieces away from the army. In particular *Fill the Stage with Happy Hours* (1966), which began triumphantly at Nottingham and then underwent some unfortunate changes of cast and re-writing before failing rather abruptly in London. All the same even in London there was a lot to be said for the play that hardly anybody cared to say. Certainly it is, in construction, rather all-over-the-place, but nearly all the parts into which it falls are very appealing. It starts out for all the world as though it is going to have a straightforward progressive plot. We meet a group of characters whose tangled relations among themselves appear to contain all sorts of dramatic possibilities. There is the slightly shady manager of a tatty provincial theatre, talking ambitiously of putting on Ibsen and *Macbeth* but actually offering a revue spiced with strip and desperately worried about whether the next Arts Council grant will come at all. (The period of the play is unspecified, but seems to be shortly after the war.) There is his wife, a great little actress now confined to keeping drunken councillors happy from behind the theatre bar. There is their strange and not very theatrically inclined son, at seventeen a big boy for his age (as several characters remark with varying degrees of lustful interest). There is Molly, their tiny, mildly demented retainer and general factotum in the theatre. And there are others: the cleaner the manager is carrying on with, the soubrette the son is carrying on with, the ageing but powerful visiting star who is determined, willy-nilly, to carry on with the son.

But as it goes on the play falls increasingly into a pattern of revue sketches, more or less successfully carried off. Particularly in the second half, where the long and in itself admirably tense and funny bedroom encounter (a little suggestive of *The Graduate* before the fact) between the star, unpierceably armoured against the world, and the boy, inexperienced but far from innocent, seems to be developed mainly for its own sake rather than for whatever it can contribute to the play as a whole. But then, this may be the impression the play deliberately sets out to create. For it is explicitly about people who are not, cannot be, changed by experience, because the only reality they know is that of the performance, the act. In its last third the play takes a very strange turn. Near the beginning the wife, Maggie, has informed us casually that she is dying; the doctor has just told her so. On and off she tells just about everybody in sight, and we assume that this is merely a part of her self-dramatization. But perhaps it is just the opposite: no one seems to take much notice, not even herself, until the end, when she suddenly stages a great Victorian deathbed scene, with family posed weeping about her and the complete works. Are we then to take it that what she has been saying all along is true? Quite possibly. But if so, nothing is changed: emotion can be really felt, Wood is perhaps suggesting, by those whose lives are spent faking emotion, only if they can continue to live their lives as so many tableaux vivants, deliberately turning life into drama. And consequently, the effects of these emotions are as slight and short-lived as the emotions they simulate on the stage – the mother's big scene serves only as one more pretext for a lecture from father to apathetic son on the theatre and what it's all about. Again, one imagines that there is a message lurking here somewhere about the relationship between reality and illusion in an actor's life, but the point is never clearly made. Probably because it goes against Wood's grain to make such points directly: and certainly the play, while curiously irritating in performance, seeming never quite to clinch its effect on any level, is still strangely haunting in the memory, and wholly individual.

It has been said that full-time writers always come round sooner or later to writing about writing, because what other experience do they have? I do not know whether we can accuse Wood of following this out on the strength of *A Bit of a Holiday* (1969), an oddly individual sour comedy about a writer who goes to Rome with his wife and children (just as Wood did on *The Adventures of Gerard*) and finds himself in the middle of an international cinematic madhouse. The play is anyway borderline to the argument, since it is not so much introspective, the writer writing about the process of writing, as outward-looking, the writer's startled response to the strange beings who inhabit an exotic and to him totally alien world. In the course of the action we meet and see through his wandering eyes a pretty crooked producer, a madly self-indulgent director, given to dressing up in extravagant Spanish costume and constantly surrounded by a retinue of miscellaneous young men, and a variety of sexy and apparently all too available young women. The writer is amused, intrigued, a little tempted and more than a little flapped by it all; his wife looks on philosophically; his children enjoy some of it and hate some. By the end of it all the 'bit of a holiday' has turned into a minor nightmare from which the whole family are grateful to escape intact. Though couched largely in terms of outrageous comic fantasy, *A Bit of a Holiday* is certainly one of the best plays ever written about film-making, capturing a surprising amount of truth in its apparent exaggerations and comic distortions (which, I may say from experience, are not as exaggerated and distorted as all that).

The same writer and his family, a lightly fictionalized image, we may take it, of Wood himself and his family, reappear in a sequel, *A Bit of Family Feeling* (1971). This time it is the writer at home with his wife, the children talked about but off-screen, and the writer's parents very much in evidence. They are staying on an extended visit while the house next door is done up for them – all at our hero's expense, though little thanks does he get for it. The action of the play all takes place in one chaotic morning in which nothing much actually happens. Peter and his wife quarrel casually about money, a friend (and ex-lover of the wife's) who is also staying drifts in and out offering them champagne for breakfast and showing off his photographic memory for the opening lines of books, and the parents little by little drive everyone mad by backing out of the limelight (and thereby causing maximum trouble for everyone concerned by showily doing everything for themselves), belittle Peter's life and achievements (while presenting an endless stream of demands for their new home) and generally do all the little, up-pin-downable things with which any parent contrives to infuriate any grown-up child. The play eventually appeared as one of a series under the general title of 'The Ten Commandments', illustrating supposedly 'Honour thy father and thy mother' – a pretty remote and backhanded illustration, one might think.

Faced with quite a bit of incomprehension, and even at times downright hostility from the critics, and – particularly as far as his only notable venture into the commercial London theatre, *Fill the Stage with Happy Hours*, is concerned – apparent indifference from the theatregoing public, Wood rather naturally felt after '*H*' a degree of disillusionment with the theatre. And of course he had already shown himself to be an extremely effective screen-writer, so there was plenty of work for him in the cinema, if not all of it, one would imagine, very satisfying creatively (though *Hadrian VII*, adapted direct from Corvo's novel rather than via the play, would seem to be something of an exception). Certainly, given Wood's extraordinary feeling for specifically theatrical effect, it is hard to imagine that he will be able to refrain for long from creating another major work for the theatre. Meanwhile, perhaps as an appetizer, he has given us the triple bill called *Welfare*, presented at the Liverpool Everyman in 1970. It consists of two plays already seen, a minor comedy called *Tie Up the Ballcock* and the rewritten version of *Meals on Wheels*, plus a new one-acter, *Labour*, which continues the themes of the other two: the relations between the old and the young, those who experienced the last war and those who did not, and the frustrations of life in an allegedly secure welfare society. This is hardly major Wood, but at least it is pleasing to know that he has not, even now, given up the theatre altogether, for surely it can no more do without him than he can do without it.

Edward Bond

One never quite knows whether it is an advantage or not for a playwright to arrive with a bang, in a storm of controversy, critical denunciations and enthusiastic counterblasts, letters to the papers from luminaries of the theatrical profession and even – that one-time accolade of the advanced dramatist, now merely an historical footnote – complete banning by the Lord Chamberlain.

On the whole, I am inclined to think that it did Edward Bond no harm when it all descended on his head over *Saved*; indeed, in terms of base (but nevertheless invaluable) publicity and the provocation of public interest, it no doubt did a lot of good. All the same, it has made him understandably retiring where personal publicity is concerned, and his unflattering views on critics in general are well known. Consequently, his plays come to us, by design, with an absolute minimum of 'background' and we have to judge them, as we should, entirely on their own merits: if they work, fine; if they don't, then neither we nor Bond can have comforting recourse to excuses based on what he says he meant, or special knowledge of his personal circumstances at the time the plays were conceived and written.

Nevertheless, it is always interesting, even if strictly speaking it shouldn't be, to know what a writer thinks of himself and his works. For this Bond has in fact provided one clear statement in the 'Author's Note' he wrote for the published text of *Saved*. And there he offers what may well be the key to most of the difficulties people – critics and the playgoing public at large – have often found in his work. 'Like most people,' he says, 'I am a pessimist by experience, but an optimist by nature, and I have no doubt that I shall go on being true to my nature. Experience is depressing, and it would be a mistake to be willing to learn from it.' Hence, presumably, his otherwise rather puzzling insistence that *Saved* is 'formally a comedy', and the sub-titling of *Narrow Road to the Deep North* as 'a comedy'. They may be comedies which come, like *Early Morning* and *The Pope's Wedding*, to the very brink of despair, but finally some sort of hope gleams through, if only because some sort of basic goodness survives indestructibly the horrors of experience and steadfastly refuses to learn from them.

This is perhaps least evidently true of the earliest play we know by Bond, *The Pope's Wedding*. This was first produced as a Sunday-night production without décor in 1962; before it we know only that Bond (born in London of working-class parents in 1935) started writing when he got out of the army and had written poetry and 'several plays'. It appears to be vaguely suggested by the subject of Raleigh Trevelyan's book *A Hermit Disclosed*, which is about the mysterious life of a man who went into retreat in the East Anglian countryside in the early years of this century and lived in virtual isolation for the rest of his life. Oddly enough, the idea seemed to exert a powerful fascination on British dramatists of the newer generation at about that time, giving rise almost simultaneously to James Saunders's *Next Time I'll Sing to You* and Henry Livings's *Jim All Alone*.

The key notion in all three plays is that the hermit provides a still centre round which everything else revolves. The Saunders is an essay in Theatre of the Absurd, using the character as a sort of ink-blot test which lends itself to an infinitude of interpretations. The Livings play is much more about the man himself, an atmosphere piece in which the central figure is taken as given and retains his mystery throughout the playwright's poetic evocation of his way of life. The Bond goes off in a rather different direction: here the subject, as it gradually crystallizes, is the relationship between a young couple on whose life the hermit impinges because the girl has an inherited responsibility of sorts for looking after him, and her husband little by little becomes obsessed with him to the exclusion of everything else, and to the point, finally, of taking his place.

In many respects *The Pope's Wedding* is comparable with the later and more familiar *Saved*. In both plays we see a young couple (married in *The Pope's Wedding*, living together in *Saved*) whose relationship is under stress; in both the man seems to represent goodness, or innocence, while it is the wife who plays around, plots and organizes. And in both the background is a life of casual violence, or at least lived in an atmosphere of violence accepted and taken for granted, among the restless, aimless young. Scopey and his eventual wife Pat both come from such a background, and are little if at all different from the other young people they know. Their day-to-day lives are occupied with fighting or various rather tough and violent forms of chaffing, interspersed with bouts of casual sex. It comes as a slight surprise, indeed, when Scopey announces in passing that he is going to marry the girl; but it is through his marriage that he begins to detach himself from his background, to emerge for us (and probably for himself too) as an individual rather than just one of a group.

And it is at this stage that, taking on Pat, he also finds that he had taken on Alen, the hermit. Alen is a cantankerous old cuss, by no means easy to get on with, let alone like. But despite his suspiciousness, his ungratefulness for services rendered, he and Scopey strike up a relationship which one could hardly call friendship but which nevertheless occupies a more and more important part in Scopey's life, until eventually he neglects his wife and is fired from his job, all in order to spend more and more time with Alen. What does he want? Hard to say. Partly no doubt to penetrate Alen's mystery. But more importantly, he just becomes fascinated by Alen's way of life – the way of withdrawal. And at the last he actually takes Alen's place, virtually becomes Alen. In the process, he has to kill Alen – at least he says so, and the playwright gives us no direct indication that we should doubt what he says.

Is that optimistic? Well, at any rate the play does not come over as pessimistic, and I think one could say of Scopey, as Bond says of Len in *Saved*, that he is naturally good, in spite of his upbringing and environment, and he remains good in spite of the pressures of the play. But he is not wholly good or easily good because then his goodness would be meaningless, at least for himself. Maybe it does, for Scopey, remain meaningless; it is something he is groping towards rather than achieving. And hence the Oedipal situation with Alen (who may or may not be his wife's father) can be resolved only by violence and death, while the equivalent situation in *Saved* between Len and his 'father-in-law' stands at the end of the play with at least the possibility of permanent contact being made, of something like friendship developing.

Perhaps that is clutching at straws, but then as Bond himself observes, so much of optimism in drama, as in life, is clutching at straws, choosing, just, to go on living even in what you feel to be a hopeless situation, and thereby signifying that you continue, however irrationally, to hope. *Saved* (1965) works entirely in these terms: its characters are at the extreme edge of their being, and are not helped in their struggle through life by their almost complete lack of intelligence. (Not that intelligence in itself solves any problems, as *Narrow Road to the Deep North* reminds us, but at least it complicates things, and complications tend to have a cushioning effect.) The relationship between Len and Pam begins with a completely casual pick-up, as we see in the first scene, Len's first arrival in Pam's home. Right away they settle down in a

pseudo-marital set-up, with Len accepted as a lodger and
Pam's usual bed-mate. If he and Pam start quarrelling very
rapidly it is only to be expected: her parents continue to live
in the same house but haven't spoken for years. Pam goes on
speaking to Len, though, and becomes more and more
savage towards him, particularly after she has had a baby –
she says, by Fred, one of a group of casually violent layabouts
she and Len know. But Len remains doggedly devoted,
especially after the baby comes, the baby being his main
reason, or perhaps his main excuse, for staying. At which
point comes the notorious scene which caused all the fuss –
that in which the baby is tormented, has excrement rubbed in
its face and is finally stoned to death by the group of layabouts, among them Fred, its alleged father.

Gradually an overall pattern of relationships is beginning
to emerge. As Len holds on grimly to his relationship with
Pam, despite her insults, so Pam tries to hold on to some sort
of relationship with Fred, even though he refuses to accept
any calls she may make upon him and, on his release from the
prison sentence he has been given for his part in the baby's
death, smartly brushes her off. Meanwhile, at home things
have been progressing somewhat. In a very tense, funny scene
Len nearly seduces Mary, Pam's mother, or she nearly
seduces him, as he is persuaded to darn a hole in her stocking
while she is still wearing it. Pam's father Harry comes in
during this scene, and afterwards is induced to speak to his
wife, breaking the silence of years. The result is a physical
attack, but that is no doubt better than silence: they are,
however elementarily, communicating again. And as a result
of this Harry begins to communicate with Len as well, in a
curious scene which apparently decides Len not to leave, as
he has been threatening, but stay on and possibly try to make
something of the household in which he lives, the pattern of
relationships of which he has somehow become a part. The
last scene is silent, all but one line – Len's 'Fetch me 'ammer'

(which nobody does) – with the three other members of the household apparently locked in wordless misery, but Bond suggests that it contains at least the seeds of hope: Len maybe is 'saved', or at least he has not lost himself, and perhaps he can do something to save the others.

The difficulty with *Saved*, it has always seemed to me, is bringing all its various elements into focus at the same time: the picture of life in the terrible family which Len enters, and the accompanying evocation of the freewheeling, casually violent and irresponsible way of life enjoyed by the group of young men Pam runs around with. In his note on the play Bond makes out quite a persuasive case for the fundamental interrelation of the two elements in the play as showing various stages of the 'Oedipus atmosphere' – the killing of the baby becoming 'the Oedipus, atavistic fury fully unleashed' as against Len's abortive tangle with Pam's father, where an Oedipal killing is sidetracked and resolved into a sort of supernatural reconciliation. Martin Esslin has elaborated a more intricate pattern of interrelationship. Reviewing the second production of the play he suggested that there is a clear pattern of cause and effect arising from lack of responsibility and understanding – the inability or refusal of Pam to respond to her child, the inability this induces (via a strong dose of aspirin) in the child to respond to the overtures of the gang, and their cumulative reaction to this: 'The baby in the pram is neglected because his mother cannot picture him as a human being like herself; the boys of the gang kill him because, having been made into an object without consciousness, they *treat* him like a mere object.'

The trouble with both explanations, it seems to me, is that they will not quite work in the theatre – or up to now they have not. Esslin's seems to me anyway to be something of a sentimentalization; Bond's own makes more sense given the nature of the total experience offered by the play, but to work properly in the theatre it probably requires a considerably less naturalistic production than either I have seen of *Saved*, emphasizing the ritual, atavistic nature of the action and cutting down the embarrassment the actors evidently feel in acting out the baby-murder more or less realistically. But then much of the play does, as Bond has said himself in one of his rare interviews, 'try to create a feeling of verisimilitude', and works very well in a naturalistic context: especially the whole of the family side of the play. In fact, everything in the play which directly involves Len, all of it which has to do with communication, can be played with perfect propriety and effectiveness this way. It is the other side of the play which causes the trouble, because it speaks in much more generalized terms. Bond says of the baby's death:

'Clearly the stoning to death of a baby in a London park is a typical English understatement; compared to the 'strategic' bombing of German towns it is a negligible atrocity, compared to the cultural and emotional deprivation of most of our children its consequences are insignificant.'

Which may be true but ignores the crucial question of the dramatic perspective in which the particular event is placed; it is not compared *within the play* to the Dresden raid or anything of the sort, but to a recognizable pattern of everyday life, and in that context, judged realistically, it cannot but seem a little arbitrary and unmotivated, set up as it were specifically to demonstrate the play's original epigraph from Blake: 'Better to kill an infant in its cradle than to nurse unacted desires', or Harry's observation to Len, relative to the war: 'Yer never killed yer man. Yer missed that. Gives yer a sense of perspective. I was one a the lucky ones.' The feeling remains that *Saved* has something urgent to say, and says it with considerable force and theatrical flair, but on two different and, it seems, practically irreconcilable levels.

In retrospect one might guess that *Saved* represents a transitional phase in Bond's work, one in which he is, more or less consciously, striving to free himself from the naturalistic style of *The Pope's Wedding*, with its meticulous notation of local country speech and recreation of a recognizably real world for its characters to live in, and reaching out towards the overtly non-realistic manner of *Early Morning* (1968). *Saved* could have made a thoroughly effective play in Bond's entirely naturalistic manner, or, seen in a different light, if he had managed to divorce it entirely from naturalism. But the text as it stands seems to me an interesting but finally unsatisfactory compromise. No question of compromise with *Early Morning*, though. Here naturalism is thrown right out of the window, and Bond is able to get straight down to what he has to say, without the necessary periphrases of superficially naturalistic drama.

Which is just as well, seeing that what he has to say is quite complex enough without the superimposition of purely technical subterfuges as well. If *The Pope's Wedding* and *Saved* can be seen as about – among other things – the corruption of man's natural innocence by 'upbringing and environment', which is to say by the forces exerted on him by abstractions like society, Christian mortality, the repressive rule of order, *Early Morning* moves a stage further, or if you like starts at the other end. The two earlier plays are about the suffering classes; *Early Morning* is about those who impose the suffering, exert the pressures. The play is a nightmare comic fantasy in which characters with historical labels – Queen Victoria, Florence Nightingale, Gladstone, Disraeli – mingle with modern characters and talk with complete equanimity about people and events which came long after their deaths. They live in a world of arbitrary, institutionalized cruelty, where cannibalism, metaphorical and later literal, is the order of the day, and the great discovery of the play's martyr-figure, Prince Arthur, is that people 'don't just hate their own life –

they hate life itself. It's a matter of conscience, like duty in the blood: they stay alive to kill.' Hence it follows that, 'What we need now is the great traitor: who kills both sides, his and theirs.'

The themes are completely consistent from *The Pope's Wedding* to *Saved* and from *Saved* to *Early Morning*. Each has an innocent (or relatively innocent) martyr-figure who with saintly or perhaps merely masochistic devotion opens himself to the worst that life has to offer. Each assumes some pervasive Oedipal situation in which humanity is seen as divided into put-upon, ill-used children and cruel, arbitrary, inscrutable parents who mete out punishments and occasional rewards with the savagery and unassailable authority of Old Testament gods. And each allows us to suppose that something may remain uncorrupted, some shred of natural goodness may survive; there is always a straw, if no more than a straw, to clutch at. It is no doubt in these terms that we should understand the indestructibility of Prince Arthur in *Early Morning*. Though his Siamese-twin brother, George, dies and is resurrected and dies again, still stubbornly attached to him; though he himself dies but cannot lose his living ability to feel pain; though he is dissected and eaten by his family in heaven, so that nothing but a neat pile of bones remains; yet, at the last, unremarked by those participating in the final cannibal feast, he comes again from his coffin, silent but undestroyed.

Right from the beginning *Early Morning* creates its topsy-turvy, War-of-the-Roses/horror comic world with ábsolute consistency. It starts with Disraeli plotting with Albert to kill Victoria and put Arthur, younger Siamese twin of George, the Prince of Wales, on the throne. Meanwhile Victoria is planning to consolidate her position by marrying George off to the current national heroine, Florence Nightingale. And in the country cannibalism has broken out: the trial is taking place of Len, accused of killing and eating another man outside the State Cinema, Kilburn High Street. As the picnic at which Victoria is to be assassinated approaches, Florence Nightingale announces that Victoria has raped her, but she does not seem too unhappy about it, and rapidly joins in Victoria's plot to dispose of Albert by poison. Disraeli continues with his plot, but it is vital for it that Arthur should be cut free from George, and Arthur refuses, so he and George escape together.

A civil war develops, and when Victoria seems to be winning, with the connivance of Len, Disraeli decides to shoot Arthur, for the good of history. Before he can do so Victoria arrives on the scene, but George dies anyway. Thereafter Arthur has to carry round with him the still-attached skeleton of George, with whom he talks though we hear only his side of the conversation. It is at this point that Arthur decides to accept the logic of endless mutual slaughter, and takes charge of the mob opposing Victoria. Victorious, he meets Victoria and Florence Nightingale again, but appears to be mad, so Victoria plots to use him to regain control. The battle is fought out in a ritual tug-of-war between the opposing armies on Beachy Head, in the course of which everyone dies and the whole cast is translated to a 'Heaven' which might just as well be called Hell (and which should, perhaps, be understood as the now mad innocent Arthur's vision of the way things are on earth). In this Heaven there is still punishment, torture and execution, but no pain; the inhabitants live literally, cannibalistically off each other, acting out even more basically the pattern of savage dog-eat-dog human relations we have seen on earth. Except for Arthur, who stubbornly continues to feel right up to the last, amid the family orgy of flesh-eating.

It is easy to accuse the play of naïvety. And of course on the level of ideas it is naïve; so are all Bond's plays. Life is not quite as simple as all that: society is not just Us and Them, the tyrants and the tyrannized, parents and children. Nor is it quite so easy for most of us to assume the position of lofty dissociation from it all that Bond seems to assume in *Early Morning*, remote from human sympathy, tolerant, if at all, because the human beings shown are as small and insignificant as the flies Queen Victoria is constantly swatting. But happily in the theatre such considerations have little to do with the case. It is not so much the abstract validity of the image presented, its power to change our own ideas on the subject, as the effectiveness of the image in itself – something which comes from the strength of the author's conviction in what he is saying, his complete commitment to his own position, however remote it may be from yours or mine. And here *Early Morning* really scores. It is not, heaven knows, a likeable play (none of Bond's, I think, is), but it packs a formidable punch in performance, and even in reading, because the strength of Bond's own obsession bludgeons us into suspending disbelief. And this despite some aspects of the plot (Queen Victoria having a lesbian affair with Florence Nightingale disguised as John Brown) which initially carry unfortunate overtones of camp fantasy far removed from Bond's methods and purposes – though it must be admitted that he very rapidly succeeds in banishing these completely from our minds.

Early Morning, of course, had even more trouble with censors and the censorious than *Saved*. And yet somehow, as has so often happened in the new drama in Britain, things were subterraneously working in Bond's favour, so that what started as incomprehensible, shocking, inducive of immediate, unthinking fury gradually came, without anyone's knowing quite how, to be accepted as, at the very least, an inescapable fact of theatrical life, so that even those who did not like Bond's plays very much found themselves agreeing to his importance. Though he had, meanwhile, written or collaborated on a number of film scripts (Volker Schloendorff's *Michael Kohlhaas*, based on a story by Kleist, Tony Richardson's

Laughter in the Dark, based on the novel by Nabokov, and most notable, Antonioni's *Blow Up*, elaborated by Bond, in collaboration, from an original story idea by Antonioni), it could hardly be said that they had aided his acceptance, since even the relatively few filmgoers on whom the technical credits impinge would find it very difficult to isolate anything specifically and unmistakably Bond's from the films as a whole. More important, obviously, was the Royal Court's dedicated espousal of his cause, culminating in their 1969 season of his plays, which even on the level of a PR operation was an undoubted triumph. But most important of all, it seems to me, is the appearance of his fourth play, *Narrow Road to the Deep North* (1968), first at Coventry, then in London, since there at last he seems to have found a form completely adapted to his content, and to have written a play which works perfectly on many levels, one at least of which almost anybody can understand and appreciate.

The principal reason for this is that in *Narrow Road to the Deep North* Bond achieves precisely the right degree of abstraction from everyday reality for his play to work as a parable without raising a lot of essentially irrelevant objections in his audience's minds. It is short, sharp, and determinedly to the point; it is also far enough removed in time and space (Japan some time vaguely in the Meiji period) not to bother us about whether it is realistic or not. Instead we are left free to respond to the play simply as a tale that is told, a succession of happenings which may, if we wish it, be interpreted in some particular sense but which do not absolutely require interpretation as a necessary means of appreciation.

In the prologue the poet Basho introduces himself to us and witnesses the abandonment of a baby by its parents on a river bank; he does nothing. When the play proper begins it is thirty years later, and Basho returns to meet Kiro, a young seeker after wisdom. He also learns about the rise meanwhile of Shogo, a local tyrant. Basho settles to a life of quiet contemplation, but is taken away by soldiers, summoned to Shogo's presence. On the way he meets Kiro and a group of young priests; Kiro has got his head stuck in a pot during some horseplay, and Basho takes Kiro and the pot along with him to Shogo. Shogo resolves Kiro's problem by the simple action of breaking the pot, despite its age and holiness. He then confides to Basho a baby, whom he tells Basho is the young emperor, son of the old emperor he killed to take power, and swears Basho to secrecy about the baby's birth. Basho is appalled by what he sees as Shogo's ruthlessness and cruelty, and advises the Prime Minister to call in the foreigners he met in the Deep North to put matters right. Meanwhile Shogo explains his ruthless and inhuman, but wholly logical, system of government to Kiro. Basho and the Prime Minister go to meet the foreigners, who prove to be a British Commodore and his evangelist sister Georgina; they are readily persuaded to attack and take Shogo's city, but Shogo and Kiro escape together in disguise.

The second act follows out the effects of the Commodore's and Georgina's rule. They prove to be even more ruthless and even more efficient than Shogo, and much to Basho's surprise Georgina admits that her religion is not sincere, but just a tool. In the course of her explanation Georgina comes up with something very close to Bond's own diagnosis of the root troubles in modern life:

GEORGINA. Shogo ruled by atrocity.

BASHO. Yes.

GEORGINA. It didn't work, because it left people free to judge him. They said: he makes us suffer and that's wrong. He calls it law and order, but we say it's crime against us – and that's why they threw spears at him. So instead of atrocity I use morality. I persuade people – in their hearts – that they

are sin, and that they have evil thoughts, and that they're
greedy and violent and destructive, and – more than anything else – that their bodies must be hidden, and that sex is
nasty and corrupting and must be secret. When they believe
all that they do what they're told. They don't judge you –
they feel guilty themselves and accept that you have the right
to judge them. That's how *I* run the city: the missions and
churches and bishops and magistrates and politicians and
papers will tell people they are sin and must be kept in order.
If sin didn't exist it would be necessary to invent it. I learned
all this from my Scottish nanny. She taught our Prime
Minister, the Queen, the Leader of the Opposition, and
everyone else who matters. They all learned politics across
her knee . . .

BASHO. You don't believe in God?

GEORGINA. Yes. But we've been talking about the devil. We
must get our priorities right. We need the devil to protect
people from themselves.

While this is going on, Kiro and Shogo have arrived in the
deep north. They are planning to hit back and recapture the
city with the help of some tribesmen, and especially with the
help of guns. Shogo carries out his plan, and massacres many
of the inhabitants. Georgina goes mad. The Commodore is
finally victorious, and announces his decision to make Basho
Prime Minister. At Shogo's trial it emerges that he was the
child whom Basho saw abandoned and did not help in the
prologue. Is Basho responsible for all that followed, in that he
did nothing either to help or kill the child? Either way, Shogo
is executed, Kiro commits harakiri, and Georgina is taken
away, stone mad, by a couple of soldiers. As Kiro plunges the
knife into his entrails a naked man climbs from the river and
berates him for not answering a cry of help. As he dries
himself, back turned, Kiro noiselessly dies.

As one would expect, *Narrow Road to the Deep North* contains
themes and ideas carried over from earlier plays, notably in
those parts which concern the Western barbarians Basho

brings in to vanquish Shogo. The evangelizing Georgina, with her cynical manipulation of the forms of Christianity as an instrument of government, a way of keeping the masses subservient, has many overtones of Bond's Queen Victoria in her speech and behaviour, and the denunciation of Christian morality in general is familiar from earlier plays, though here more pointedly and economically expressed. (It is worth noting, however, that Georgina is to some extent humanized by contradictory traits like sympathy for the murdered children, and that it is these contradictions which ultimately drive her mad.) Familiar too is the character of Kiro, another innocent seeking contact with the worst of the world; and if he finally despairs and kills himself, the naked swimmer who at that very moment emerges from the river carries with him unmistakable overtones of innocence new-born. Basho too fits in, as the inhuman dweller in the ivory tower, who fails in humanity at the crucial moment (if he had saved the child in the prologue presumably the rest of the play would never happen) and then temporizes, accommodates, reacts when he does – to preserve his own peace of mind – too hastily and wrong, all in the cause of some deluding abstract ideal of the dedicated life of poetry. If anyone is the villain of the play, he is.

But the play also marks a new stage in Bond's mastery of his material and his ability to display it to best advantage. The dialogue is pared to the bone, and placed with a poetic wit and economy which shows the hand of a master stage craftsman – something which before one would hardly have put in the forefront of Bond's qualifications as a dramatist. And above all, the play bears the mark on every page of Bond's maturing as a dramatic thinker, his increasing awareness of the complexities of life and moral decision. He has remarked of this play that 'There are good things and bad things in almost everybody in the play, and it is the incidents which speak for me.' He has said much the same of earlier plays, but this time the intention is really carried through to complete achievement.

Bond's next dramatic work after *Narrow Road to the Deep North* was the one-act play, *Black Mass*, written for the Anti-Apartheid Movement's commemoration of the tenth anniversary of Sharpeville in March 1970. In it Christ comes down from the cross and poisons the communion wine about to be taken by the South African Prime Minister. In retaliation for the minister's death Christ is banished from the church, and his place on the cross taken by young uniformed policemen in endless succession. In the same period Bond has also written the English dialogue for an Italian film, *The Nun of Monza*, another screenplay, *Walkabout*, based on a novel by James Vance Marshall, and, in collaboration with Keith Hack, an adaptation of Brecht's *Die Rundköpfe und die Spitzköpfe* (*The Roundheads and the Peakheads*) – itself originally based on *Measure for Measure* – which has in this version been re-interpreted in terms of present-day Britain.

And in the meantime Bond has been working on a new major play, which he describes as a version of *King Lear* without King Lear. A production announced for April 1971 failed to materialize, but instead we were given a new short piece, *Passion*, staged by the Royal Court as part of a Festival of Life organized by C.N.D. In it a soldier has died and his mother petitions the queen for his return just as she gave him to the queen when war broke out. But he has meanwhile been transformed into a statue, which is due to be unveiled. During the ceremony the explosion of the ultimate bomb destroys civilization utterly, but the Queen and the Prime Minister survive, heedless of the intervention of Christ and Buddha; perhaps after all nothing has really changed. The playlet is a sort of companion piece to *Black Mass*, working in the same broad strokes of allegory and heavy irony; it is a kind of *pièce d'occasion* which Bond does better than anyone. But meanwhile his King Lear play is eagerly awaited; his starting-point for it, that Lear is the character in Shakespeare who tells all the lies, and so the story is much more interesting without him, sounds encouraging. After *Saved* one might have been permitted to doubt Bond's ability to tackle such a theme; after *Early Morning* and *Narrow Road to the Deep North* he seems ready for anything.

Tom Stoppard

It would be tempting to label Tom Stoppard as the intellectual among our young playwrights, if 'intellectual' did not always tend, in the British theatre anyway, to have the ring of a dirty word. Also, he does deny very firmly that it's true: however precisely calculated his plays look, he insists that when he starts writing them he has no clearer idea of exactly where they are going, or exactly how they will get there, than the most innocent, uninformed member of a first-night audience. Nevertheless, the most striking, and most strikingly individual, effect Stoppard's plays make comes from their evident concern with structure, with overall pattern. Where other dramatists produce big, untidy effects, spilling out their materials generously, and often too generously, with little apparent concern for economy, concentration and scrupulous adaptation of means to ends, Stoppard works by neatness, precision, a meticulous tying-in of loose ends. He professes to mistrust most of all the arbitrary in art, the play which works as linear experience from moment to moment; he likes and works towards the feeling of completeness as one piece after another falls into place, and finds it very important for him that the structure of his plays should lock finally into a clear pattern with a 'clunk' at the end.

This obsession, almost, with dramatic syntax is evident even in the very earliest work of Stoppard's we know, *Enter a Free Man*. This was, in fact, the very first play he wrote, while he was working as a reporter on the *Western Daily Press* in Bristol; it was first produced on television as *A Walk on the Water* in November 1963, when he was 26, and went virtually unnoticed at a time when all the most spectacular dramas were going on in the real world (it was just after the assassination of President Kennedy). It turned up in Hamburg the following year in its original form as a stage play, and finally, after the success of *Rosencrantz and Guildenstern are Dead*, it appeared in the West End in March 1968, as *Enter a Free Man*. Presumably it had undergone some revision in the meantime, but if decidedly hazy recollections of the original television production serve, the outlines of the play remain constant, and it is in the outlines that the Stoppardness of Stoppard is most readily recognizable.

In comparison with his later work, *Enter a Free Man* is surprisingly straightforward and realistic-seeming. It is much more firmly founded on character, gleefully explored for its own sake, than any of his later glittering constructions. The character in question being of course that of George Riley, failed inventor and fantasist extraordinary. His inventions are of the order of envelopes with gum on both sides of the flap, so that you can turn them inside out and use them twice, and indoor rain for watering the plants, which his stoical wife persists in watering with a watering-can anyway. He is now middle-aged, '. . . no longer handsome, features that are perhaps more interesting than beautiful . . .' as he cheerfully observes, and he is getting to the end of his tether. Or he seems to be. But his tether is considerably longer than he thinks: his gift for dramatizing even the dullest, most everyday situation, his constant weaving of hopeful fantasies in expectation of the one big breakthrough which will transform his life, elasticate it to the point where in fact he can take anything and spring back ready for more.

In other words, we know even as he announces that he is chucking it all up, leaving his stolidly unresponsive wife and amiably sceptical daughter, that he will be back before the play is done, that the action will be circular. The great strength of the play as Stoppard writes it is that he chooses to go along with this realization, to play it up for us instead of playing it down. Another writer, given the same basic material, the same dramatic situation, might have tried to build up artificial suspense by keeping us wondering – or trying to keep us wondering – whether this time it's for keeps, this time he really means what he says. But not Stoppard. He keeps us perfectly aware that his play is built like a goldfish bowl, in which the principal character may swim round and round, showing himself off, but from which he has no real ability, and probably not even any real desire, to escape, even if he chooses to nurture from time to time the illusion of his own freedom.

In comparison with Stoppard's later plays, though, *Enter a Free Man* remains a little crude, a little obvious. The clunk does come at the end, as George returns to the *status quo*, making a show of accepting that there has been some little something wrong with all his inventions but still, even as he ostensibly plans to get an ordinary job again tomorrow, hankering after the idea of being an inventor. But the built-in irony is a bit too pat, just as before George's wife's speech showing that under it all she knows what is going on and feels for George ('. . . you don't ask yourself what it costs him to keep his belief in himself – to come back each time and start again – and it's worth keeping, it's the last thing he's got . . .'), comes a bit too close to the stock sentimental gesture. George himself remains an appealing comic creation, a part that might have been written for Michael Hordern, who played it in the West End, but the neatness of the play which contains him, though pointing to Stoppard's later passion for pattern-making, lacks the intricacy of point and paradox which seems necessary really to fire his imagination.

Like so many young dramatists, Stoppard found his best platform as a beginner in radio and television rather than the theatre. He also wrote a novel, *Lord Malquist and Mr Moon* (1965), mainly, he says, because the publisher was mad enough to want to commission a novel from him and it seemed like a good idea at the time. Actually, once embarked on it he rather enjoyed it, but he feels that his natural sympathies are entirely with the drama, in one form or another. At the same time he wrote two fifteen-minute radio plays, *The Dissolution of Dominic Boot* and *M is for Moon among Other Things* (1965), three short television plays, *A Separate Peace* (1966), *Teeth* and *Another Moon Called Earth* (1967), and two more substantial radio plays, *If You're Glad I'll Be Frank* (1966) and *Albert's Bridge* (1967).

Already in these the characteristics which we would now think of as Stoppard's own personal property are beginning to emerge. *Teeth*, for example, is a piece of his fanatically neat, unashamedly artificial comic plotting, about a dentist who manages (horror situation *par excellence!*) to get his wife's lover at his mercy in the chair, and subject him to refined torture for half an hour with the assistance of his nurse, who happens to be the victim's wife. *A Separate Peace* is a sad little play about a man who signs himself into a private hospital one night because he wants to be nursed, looked after, required to do nothing, explain nothing. It seems perfectly logical: the only thing that worries the staff is that he isn't ill. What he needs is a hospital for the healthy, but clearly that is a notion which doesn't enter into anybody else's calculations, so they worry round him, trying to find an ailment of which to cure him. Eventually they find out who he is, trace his family and get him all ready to 'connect' again. At which he promptly moves out, in search of another 'separate peace'. *Another Moon Called Earth* also reflects Stoppard's penchant for the rigidly logical following-out of an argument from a mad premise – or at any rate one which seems mad to the world at large. A conventional married man tries desperately to make sense of a situation in which his wife has retired permanently to bed since the landing of the first man on the moon, receiving in dubious circumstances a strange man who may or may not be her doctor and driving her old nanny to suicide, while she tries to explain to him that the landing on the moon puts the earth in a totally new perspective which may invalidate all our received standards of morality and conventions of everyday behaviour.

Radio, perhaps because its audiences are normally smaller and more specialized, seems to have brought out the best in Stoppard. *If You're Glad I'll be Frank* reflects a slightly different side of his talent from the television plays; a metaphysical fantasy about a bus-driver who believes – correctly, as it transpires – that he has identified in the voice of the talking clock his long-lost wife Gladys, it is full of details both absurd and Absurd. The idea of the bus-driver so tied to his route and schedule that he can pursue his inquiries after his wife only in seconds snatched from the timetable, with his bus temporarily parked outside full of impatient passengers, is obviously a nice farcical notion, if no more, while the idea of someone passionately trying to summon up some personal response from the voice of TIM has the same sort of idiotic inconsequence as Kirby Groom-kirby's attempts to teach speak-your-weight machines to sing the Hallelujah Chorus in *One Way Pendulum*.

But if the basic ideas are funny simply in terms of a sort of Goon Show freewheeling fantasy, what Stoppard chooses to do with them is far more methodical. The whole play is in fact about Time, and about man's subservience to Time. Both Frank and Gladys are placed in a classic Theatre of the Absurd situation, as agents transformed into objects; deprived of almost all free will, they function mechanically within a totally artificial, inhuman framework – Frank with his endless, unvarying bus schedules, Gladys permanently at her telephone informing anyone and everyone of the precise time without variation, without interruption. Nothing in the play is purely arbitrary, nothing is there just for a quick laugh. A lot of it is very funny, but the ruthless logic with which it is all worked out, not to mention the fitful gleams of poetry in Gladys's strange interior monologues, gives it a nightmarish intensity one cannot quite explain. For the first time Stoppard is producing something which is all his own, not at all like anyone else.

And then came *Rosencrantz and Guildenstern are Dead*. This play too had a rather chequered history. The first whisper of it was a one-act farce in verse, which Stoppard now hopes and believes has disappeared for good. Next, he started again, this time to write a full-length play about Rosencrantz and Guildenstern, and what sort of lives they led in their own right in the intervals of being attendant gentlemen at the beck and call of the great, which would summon them for brief moments out of the shadows into the glare of dramatic attention. Before he had properly finished the play he let it, or as much of it as he had then written, be performed on the Edinburgh Festival fringe in 1966. The Royal Shakespeare Company more or less commissioned him to write the last act, but then for some reason decided not to produce the play, and finally it went on at the National Theatre in April 1967. Its reception by critics and public was little short of ecstatic, and almost overnight Stoppard found himself accepted on all sides as the new white hope of British theatre. Some rather unlikely things happened: film companies acquired the rights of *Lord Malquist and Mr Moon* and of *Rosencrantz and Guildenstern* itself, neither of which would seem on the face of it exactly a natural for the cinema; even *Albert's Bridge*, Stoppard's next radio play, has been bought for filming by the man who set up *Yellow Submarine*, to be made with a lot of animation, though not actually as a cartoon.

It all sounds like success – success in the most basic commercial terms as well as any more elusive, theoretical kind. And so, evidently, it is. But there can have been few more improbable launching-pads for such success, even in the unpredictable days of the 'new drama' and after, than

Rosencrantz and Guildenstern are Dead. It is a long play in which virtually nothing happens: as soon as we meet the principals for the first time, playing some interminable game of coin-tossing, which defies all the rules of chance by coming up heads eighty-five times in a row, we know (primed with Beckett and all that crush) that Godot will never come, nothing will ever change, the two will remain perforce waiting in the wings for the rest of their lives, never quite grasping what is happening centre-stage of life. They can perhaps make a choice of some kind, decide to act instead of merely being acted upon; but if they do, they will be denying their essential nature, and will be able to assert their own existence only by independently choosing to extinguish it.

Which is fair enough: a pattern of Stoppard's imposed upon, or neatly dovetailed with, the pre-existing pattern of Shakespeare's play. In *Hamlet* Rosencrantz and Guildenstern are a couple of characters so unimportant that Olivier could remove them from his film without any noticeable difficulty and with almost no one regretting their departure. They are the perennial 'attendant lords', 'friends to the duke' and what-have-you who lurk on the sidelines of drama ready to receive confidences from the principals, carry out commissions and do any minor dirty work that happens to be going. But what are their private lives like? Do they have any? Stoppard thinks not. They live, suspended in existential doubt, on the fringes of life. They never know what's happening, who is who and what is what. Occasionally they witness puzzling snatches of big events going on around them (the scenes of Shakespeare's play in which they figure), but their attempts to interpret them are limited and half-hearted. They recognize, in spite of themselves, that life, like laughter is always in the next room. In the end they go so far as to make a choice, or at least acquiesce in the choice of another, but it is only death that they choose, a death which will at last define and give shape to their pointless, shapeless lives.

The conception is cool, cunning, and intellectual: not for Stoppard the romantic inventions of those who choose to speculate on the nature of King Lear's wife, the number of children Lady Macbeth had, or what happens next to Katharina and Petruchio – the whole point of his play is to reinforce the strict classical viewpoint that dramatic characters do not have any independent, continuing existence beyond the confines of what their inventor chooses to tell us about them. This, it seems to me, Stoppard's play does with great skill and virtuosity; but, it is very evidently the working out of an intellectual, almost one might say a scholarly, conceit, with I would have thought little to capture the interest of a non-specialist audience once the pattern has become patent. It is not, to put it mildly, a play mad with too much heart.

And yet I am obviously wrong in this assessment; the play has not only had great success on its home ground, but has gone on to almost universal success abroad. This proves, if anything does, that audiences are not by any means so impervious to the appeal of writing which sets out to work on them primarily by way of their intelligence as we always, much too loftily, tend to assume. I am sure that the National Theatre was the ideal place for the play first to appear, because with a National Theatre audience it could take for granted an acquaintance with the root material (*Hamlet*, that is), and considerably less acquaintance with even the most hallowed classics of the Theatre of the Absurd. Taking its public gently by the hand, it confidently, excitingly led them from the known to the unknown, and gave them a good lively time along the way. There is no denying the ingenuity with which Stoppard spins out his material, or the skill with which he works in such fragments of *Hamlet* as concern his own non-heroes. The play is written in brisk, informal prose, suitable for those waiting in the wings, while Shakespeare's verse marks off the brief incursions of a larger life into the colourless, mystifying existence of the principals. A lot of Stoppard's dialogue is agile and funny, and his characterization of the couple as a sort of Holmes/Watson double act, one dashing ahead (if in no direction he wishes to travel) and the other lagging doggedly behind, is fetching. But I still feel that for audiences more thoroughly familiar with the more advanced sections of modern theatre than the average National Theatre audience, the play is too long-drawn-out for its material, that too long a time elapses between our becoming aware of the play's drift and its actual accomplishment.

Even so, *Rosencrantz and Guildenstern are Dead* definitively marked the arrival of a dramatist not quite like any other. All Stoppard's works since have been relatively slight, at least in terms of physical scale. There was *Albert's Bridge*, which won the Italia Prize for 1968, the longish one-act comedy *The Real Inspector Hound* (1968), a spy drama for television *Neutral Ground* (1968), a radio play – originally for schools – *Where Are They Now?* (1970), and most recently a companion piece for *The Real Inspector Hound*, *After Magritte* (1970). Apart from *Neutral Ground*, they are all comedies, though all with at least a touch of that metaphysical unease which is Stoppard's trademark. *Neutral Ground* goes off in a rather different direction, coming out a bit like a cross between T. S. Eliot and John Le Carré. The Eliot comes in with the basic idea, which is a transposition (rather satisfyingly ingenious if you know the original) of the *Philoctetes* of Sophocles to a modern setting; the Le Carré with the setting chosen, the situation of a grubby, down-at-heel spy (called Philo, of course), contemptuously cast off by his former employers, who now discover they need him and send two emissaries, based on the cunning Ulysses and the fumbling but decent Neoptolemus, to lure their difficult, obstinate and now aggrieved man back. The result is quite holding, but somehow ordinary: character, one suspects, is not in itself one of Stoppard's strong points – only character as one of the pieces in a complicated pattern. And the pattern here is really only the intellectual conceit of redefining Sophocles in modern terms, which hardly turns out to be enough.

The patterns of the other four plays could hardly be more complicated. *Albert's Bridge* all takes place on and around one of those bridges which, *Believe It or Not* used to tell us, are always in the process of being painted, because by the time the painters reach one end it is time to start repainting the other. The drama here comes from some intricate mathematical juggling. If it takes four men two years, reasons an official, it would be more economical to use an eight-year paint and fire three men. This is, of course, a logical fallacy, since it means that the far end, coated with two-year paint, will have to wait eight years before it is repainted. But the course of action, once initiated, cannot be reversed except by a drastic step: bringing in so many painters that the whole bridge can be repainted in one day. Only drawback is that under the weight of so many people the bridge collapses. The fantasy is beautifully worked out in terms of the medium (radio), achieving a very happy balance between the rigid formal structure of ideas and the appealing character of Albert, the intellectual painter who is left in solitary charge of Clufton Bay Bridge during the play's middle section. *Where Are They Now?* is a very slight piece about a school reunion which makes quite ingenious play with different eras coexisting in memory and association, the patterns of relationship between teachers and boys, seniors and juniors, never really changing despite changed circumstances and constantly renewing itself in new generations. It is cleverly done, but seems to have little to say beyond the most superficial evoking of a widely shared experience.

In *The Real Inspector Hound* and *After Magritte* pattern is all. Both involve an element sending up the conventions of detective fiction: the first imagines two drama critics (well, one critic, Birdboot, and one second-string, Moon, to be precise) watching an absurd tabloid thriller on stage. Little by little they become involved with what is happening on stage, first by Birdboot recommending a young actress in a minor role to Moòn's attention, and thus inspiring in Moon some nasty suspicions, then as their personal dramas (Birdboot's relations with his wife, Moon's passionate hope that his number one, Higgs, will die and hand on the job to him) get inextricably mixed up with the stage thriller's search, via Inspector Hound, for a homocidal maniac stalking the marshes around isolated Muldoon Manor. Eventually, after Hound – if Hound it be – has arrived on the scene, Moon in a fit of irritation dashes on to the stage to answer a ringing telephone, and finds that the call is for Birdboot. Trapped on stage when the action resumes, Birdboot has to try to play his part in it. To make matters worse, he discovers that the body on stage is in fact Moon's superior Higgs. Moon takes Hound's place as Birdboot has taken Simon's, while Simon and Hound occupy their seats and pontificate from the stalls. It all fits together with a sort of demented clockwork precision, but Stoppard insists that when he started work on it (goaded by Michael Codron, who wanted a companion piece to another one-act play), he had only a few pages of goonish humour to go on and no idea that the body would be Higgs, let alone that Magnus ('the wheelchair-ridden half-brother of her ladyship's husband Lord Albert Muldoon who, ten years ago, went out for a walk on the cliffs and was never seen again') would turn out to be the real Inspector Hound, Albert and Macafferty, Moon's own jealous stand-in, who stands in relation to him as he does to Higgs.

After Magritte is if anything even more fiendishly complicated. When it opens the Harrises have a slight problem. Well, more of a misunderstanding, you might call it, since after all it doesn't matter a damn. The thing is, he is convinced that the figure they saw after leaving the Magritte exhibition at the Tate Gallery was an old man with a white beard, in pyjamas, carrying a tortoise, while she just knows beyond contradiction that it was a limping footballer with a football under his arm. It is all very well for her husband to point out that white-bearded footballers with a limp and probably blind to boot, since the character in question was carrying a white stick, are hardly likely to find many calls being made on their services; Thelma is impervious to sarcasm, and anyway, she adds, it wasn't a beard, it was shaving foam. Mother is not much help either (she must be somebody's mother, but neither of the Harrises is quite sure whose): as far as she is concerned it was an escaped convict in striped prison uniform carrying a crocodile-skin handbag under his arm.

It might sound from this summary of the situation as though Stoppard has chosen this time to do a Simpson. Especially since the scene is promptly invaded by a demented policeman, Chief Inspector Foot ('Not Foot of the Yard?' queries Harris brightly), with an elaborate theory all worked out which fingers the Harrises as accessories in a postulated robbery involving a one-legged black-face minstrel, and possibly as murderers as well. Foot works with ruthless logic from a basically idiotic premise, just as so many of Simpson's characters do, and the somewhat strenuous exchanges of absurdities which result from his appearance in the Harrises' living-room just as they are preparing to compete in an evening's ballroom dancing have a decidedly Simpsonish flavour. But there are other things in the play. For instance, you might wonder what a couple like this were doing at a Magritte exhibition; Inspector Foot certainly does. The answer is simple: Mother is a devotee of the tuba, playing it enthusiastically herself and following up every possible reference to the instrument of her choice. So of course, having heard that tubas figured in the paintings of Magritte, she had to be taken along to look. She was disappointed though: as she gives us to understand in one of the play's funniest patches, for a serious tuba-fancier Magritte leaves a lot to be desired.

Further – and here the play becomes distinctively the work of Stoppard – the apparent surrealistic absurdities of the action are not purely arbitrary. What for Simpson would be the material of a free, anarchic fantasy turns out in this play to be as rigidly patterned and organized as a crossword puzzle. Stoppard proudly insists that there is a perfectly logical explanation for everything in the play, and he is doubtless right, though no one could be expected to catch all the detailed correspondences at one viewing. The mysterious figure, for instance, who does matter a damn because he seems to be the only witness to a vital stage in the Harrises' supposed crime, is eventually explained by something Inspector Foot says – though he himself remains sublimely unaware that he was himself the occasion of so much argument and speculation – and all the other details fall into place in the same way. Perhaps, to be really carping, they all fall into place a bit too neatly, though Stoppard denies that he knew from the start how everything would fit in, finding out only bit by bit as he went along. In its obsessive neatness *After Magritte* has a lot in common with Stoppard's other works: there is always a dangerous tendency for them to confine, or seem to confine, their ideas too rigidly to a pre-arranged pattern, to rule out those elements of the arbitrary and the accidental which give life to the drama. In the case of *After Magritte* the intention was to do no more than divert and tease a lunch-time audience for forty minutes, and that it did quite splendidly.

As for the rest, we may accept fairly happily Stoppard's insistence that intellect is not the prime motive-force in his work, just as we recognize that there are passages in it, notably in the monologues of Gladys in *If You're Glad I'll be Frank* and Albert in *Albert's Bridge*, which are beyond the reach of intellectual calculation. Perhaps the doubts I feel to some extent about all Stoppard's work boil down, rather surprisingly, to a feeling that he lacks a sort of fundamental seriousness as a playwright, that his ideas remain, in the Coleridgean definition, on the level of fancy rather than imagination. But all the same, it is pleasing to note that there is at least one young dramatist who, whatever the starting-point of his dramatic work, feels that intelligence and conscious art in the shaping of his material are necessary, are indeed a positive source of inspiration, rather than some dangerous outsider, to be tangled with very much at his peril.

Peter Terson

'I think anyone writing about my plays should see the paintings I do while I'm working on them. I just slosh the paint on, as boldly and simply as you like, and the subjects are all very simple and obvious: A MAN, A STREET and so on. I don't know why I do them, and when I've done them I just chuck most of them away. I think my plays are very much like that. I suppose I must be some sort of crazy primitive or something.'

Thus Peter Terson on his working methods. And though in general I would deeply mistrust anyone who defines himself as a primitive – even if he is sincere he is almost sure to be wrong – in this case I think the diagnosis is probably correct. At least, I am sure that the strengths of Terson's works are all the strengths of the primitive (the same goes for his weaknesses), and that his most effective plays work on us as they do precisely because he can still deal unaffectedly with great, simple issues in great, simple terms. 'A man with a fear of sophistication,' Irving Wardle once called him. True enough, but if he fears it, it is because he finds little temptation in it for himself, and knows perfectly well that whatever benefit it may be to other writers, to him it would be no use at all.

Sophistication, of course, is not the same thing as subtlety. Though Terson doubts his ability to write 'the subtle, psychological stuff', in fact his plays, if cheerfully elementary on the level of ideas, are full of strange intuitive insights into the characters and their mental processes. I would stress the 'intuitive' – it must be literally true that Terson is not consciously aware of what he is doing in his plays while he is writing them. And certainly none of them seems to come from analysis of the subject and an intellectual elaboration of a pattern as a basis for the action. One feels that the plays just happen, like life itself, incident being added to incident by some sort of natural accretion until some overall shape emerges. Or, perhaps, doesn't emerge: Terson admits very readily that he is a hit or miss writer, writing perhaps as many as eight plays which don't work for every one that does reach production. ('My plays fundamentally either have a workable idea or they don't: I have a fair notion myself which are which when I've written them, but I depend heavily on other people, particularly Peter Cheeseman and Michael Croft, to tell me for sure.')

Born in 1932, Peter Terson began writing when he was twenty-five, and has been writing with fanatical persistence and determination ever since. He says that he had 'strange urges' towards writing while still at school, but they got submerged during his years at the local technical college in Newcastle-upon-Tyne and his national service in the RAF, to surface, disconcertingly, around 1957 when he was married and working as a games teacher. The immediate impetus came from the birth of his first child, and consequent long nights sitting up with a fretful baby. First, Terson found himself embarked on a vast, shapeless novel written laboriously in longhand in the intervals of boiling milk, rocking and tucking in. Pretty soon he decided there was no future in this, and started instead 'just writing down the chat' – and so the playwright was born. To his surprise and gratification, the BBC bought options right away on the first two scripts he wrote, but nothing further came of that, and eventually they were dropped (quite rightly, he now says) on the grounds that they just needed too much work doing on them. There followed seven years of sparetime writing, with playscripts emerging in endless succession, and rejection slips piling relentlessly up, until, as a result of reading a piece about Peter Cheeseman and his work at Stoke, Terson was inspired to send him his latest play, *The Runaway*. Cheeseman didn't like it, but was sufficiently interested to pursue the matter, and the result was Terson's first performed play, *A Night to Make the Angels Weep*, done by the Victoria Theatre in 1964.

The meeting with Peter Cheeseman was a turning-point in Terson's career for more than the obvious reason: that he had at last found a theatrical outlet for his work and a sympathetic director. For Terson is virtually unique among our dramatists in that he does not believe he functions at all efficiently in isolation, writing a finished text in his study, which will then be produced essentially as it stands, with only minor modifications suggested in rehearsal. He says that he dislikes the actual process of writing, because he dislikes the loneliness of it – which is why he could never be a novelist. The pleasure and inspiration of play-writing come for him, primarily, from contact with actors, with a director, with the whole business of realizing the words on paper in action. Thus, nearly all his plays, even when completely written out in what appears to be a final form before rehearsals begin, have been extensively reworked with the production group, Terson regarding what he has written alone as merely the starting-point.

Hence, the influence exerted on him by Peter Cheeseman and Michael Croft in particular, and more generally by the Victoria Theatre, the National Youth Theatre and their methods of work, has been of radical importance in the development of Terson's style and in the detailed shaping of his plays as we know them in performance and in print. In his introduction to the published version of *The Apprentices* (1968), for instance, Michael Croft goes into much illuminating detail about how, precisely, the play was changed and elaborated in production according to the specific needs of the National Youth Theatre at that time, its strong and weak points, with roles being dropped or created largely in terms of the players available, and developments in the ideas behind the play coming up constantly through the interaction of the actors, director and writer. In Terson's National Youth Theatre plays particularly, the process of creation would seem to have been continuous right up to opening night: with *Fuzz* (1969), Terson has scarifying stories of writing the last scene in its final version the morning of the opening, and having the lines learnt an hour before the curtain went up. Even if that was a little too much of a good thing, in general Terson seems to enjoy writing in such circumstances, and feels that his best work is done that way.

It is perhaps not altogether surprising that these two continuing professional involvements should have brought out two different sides of Terson's talents. Partly it is in response to the very different special aptitudes of the two companies, and partly, no doubt, because of the very different temperaments of Peter Cheeseman and Michael Croft sparking off Terson's invention. Very roughly and summarily, one could say that the Stoke plays are deliberately smaller in scale, quieter, and closer-knit, while the National Youth Theatre plays are big, showy, loud and energetic: several of the Stoke plays are rural in their background, and generally backward-looking, while the NYT plays are defiantly urban and of the here-and-now. It is the second group of plays which has made Terson's name nationally and internationally (partly, of course, from the elementary fact that they are the ones which have been staged not only in London and seen by all the national critics, but also in Europe), but Terson feels that fundamentally they are much less him, less reflective of his own private personality and preoccupations, than the Stoke plays. And indeed, the instant excitements of their production apart, *Zigger Zagger*, *The Apprentices*, *Fuzz* and *Spring-Heeled Jack* do seem in many respects less substantial than the Vale of Evesham plays which first brought Terson forward in Stoke.

I should perhaps explain that for several years of his teaching career and life as an unknown, unproduced writer,

Terson lived in the Vale of Evesham, a fruit-growing district in the shadow of Housman's Bredon Hill and cheek-by-jowl with the Black Country. To many it is a pleasing rural retreat, but Terson found it 'closed in, especially at blossom time, and claustrophobic and frightening', and attributes to this feeling the fact that all the plays he wrote set in the Vale of Evesham 'have this element of fear and repression' in them. (Presumably he is not alone in this feeling, incidentally, since David Rudkin's *Afore Night Come* is also set in the Vale of Evesham.) The plays of Terson's which come in this group are *A Night to Make the Angels Weep* (1964), *The Mighty Reservoy* (1964), *Mooney and his Caravans* (televised 1966, staged 1967), *All Honour Mr Todd* (1966) and *I'm in Charge of These Ruins* (1966).

Though varied in the details of their subject-matter, they recognizably form a cycle. The same themes, in various forms, echo through all of them. Funnily enough, though, it was the 'natural' side of Evesham, suffocating in a sea of blossom, that Terson found most sinister. In his country plays, as a rule, nature seems to be somehow right, as against the menacing onslaught of mechanization, of town people with town ways. Change is rarely seen as anything but evil, and old times are nearly always good old times. Perhaps the most extreme instance of these attitudes comes in the earliest of the plays to appear, *A Night to Make the Angels Weep*. Here the central situation involves the ambitions of a squire called Saxon to reassume the position in local society which the lord of the manor once had, and, rather more surprisingly, the support he gets in the village to make him suppose that this may in fact happen. Admittedly, the motives of Saxon's chief supporters, the wild boys Dig and Sin, are left rather obscure – we can never be sure how far they are sincere, and how far they are playing some mysterious game of their own. In particular, there is their hostility towards the disreputable Dezzel, alleged fount of all evil in the village, and his sidekick

Herbo to be taken into account. And the final result of their scheming is to lead Saxon into killing Dezzel, who seems to be attacking Saxon's daughter Vanessa. Maybe it is the squirearchy taking its revenge on the rebellious peasantry, but if so the gesture is too belated: now Saxon will be simply accused of murder. And just as well, perhaps, though Terson's attitude to change as such is always ambiguous, and tends to be hostile.

The play is constructed loosely in scenes which alternate the free-living rustics Dezzel and Herbo with the convention-bound squire, his family and his supporters. Within the rustic scenes a lot of play is made with simple images, particularly the contrast between the stifling hollow where the village lies and the hilltops where a man can breathe. The town and town visitors figure mainly as an unseen menace: rich businessmen coming down with their tarts for dirty week-ends in caravans. And yet acceptance by rich week-enders seems to be becoming a last refuge, a fantasy, and one might well, not unfairly, extract from the play as a whole the message that the feudal way has more validity, more present reality even, than the sophisticated, townified ways which look like the one, poor alternative.

Perhaps this is an unduly simplistic reading of *A Night to Make the Angels Weep*, but other plays in the cycle give colour to the interpretation. In *All Honour Mr Todd*, for example, the intruders digging a vast sewer are seen very much as a bad thing – at least within the context of the rural community whose life they disrupt. And though obviously one could think of other more sympathetic views on the subject, since we are offered none of them within the play, hostility remains obstinately the angle from which Terson forces us to see the sewermen. In this case the machines seem to win out: the villagers go over to the newcomers, deserting the hero whose settled, traditional views of village life prove no match for the corrupting excitements of the modern world.

In *I'm in Charge of These Ruins*, the images are even more elementary: to one side the glowering new power-station which dominates the landscape: to the other the crumbling remains of a medieval castle, watched over by a pathetic, almost equally ruinous old guide. Of course, the power-station could represent the good in modern life, the practical advantages, even the austere beauty. But watching the play there seems little doubt that Terson's sympathies are with the ruins, the good old days crumbling into dust to be replaced by nothing very appealing, certainly nothing warm, human, idiosyncratic.

The argument is brought down to personalities in *Mooney and His Caravans*. Some critics have complained that in the other plays of this period the characterization is elementary, and that is true, though not necessarily a subject for complaint: Terson's characterization is of a piece with his overall dramatic method, which works in bold, simple effects more akin to those of the morality play or the Jonsonian comedy of humours than to anything more modish and up-to-the-minute. When he wants to he can move in closer and give us more detail. In *Mooney and His Caravans* he proves it, though in a rather surprising context. Basically, this is a scarifying comedy about a town couple who move into the country, as they think – in point of fact, to a caravan site run like a voluntary concentration camp – in search of escape and a return to nature. Everything goes wrong, partly because they are exploited, but also, more importantly, because Charley, the feeble husband, lets himself be exploited. The play charts the course of their relationship with each other, and with the world outside, the world of Mooney, the rustic slum landlord, entirely in terms of a duologue between husband and wife, in six scenes.

Obviously, this is not exactly the easy way to do it, since with little visible action and no other characters to diversify the effect, the dramatist must come up with something in the

way of character penetration to keep the play alive. This
Terson does: though most of the agonies and humiliations
suffered by the couple are pretty predictable, their reactions
to them are not, nor is the way that what happens to them
affects their relationship. Unexpectedly, the worse things get
for Charley (despite all his attempts to laugh off or claim
happy complicity in his own humiliation), the closer Mave
draws to him. And even though they represent the town, their
troubles arouse our sympathy: the play perhaps represents a
further stage in the corruption of the country, which has here
already gone so far downhill that it is reduced to a trap into
which the townsman will inevitably fall, and all the more
completely the more well-meaning he is, the more confident
in the restorative powers of the nature he foolishly expects to
find waiting for him in the countryside.

But then, too, Charley and Mave are exiles, excluded from
the good things, from participation in the world which moves
and works as smoothly as a well-oiled machine. And as such,
they have an immediate call on Terson's sympathy and
understanding. He says that as a person he always feels
himself to be left out, alone on the fringes of a world in which
everyone else seems to fit, to be well-adjusted, to know where
he is going. And so, as a person and as a writer, he immediately establishes a bond of sympathy with others in some way
left out: alcoholics, nuts pursuing some solitary obsession like
the railway enthusiasts in his television play *The Last Train
through the Harecastle Tunnel*, little men building St Paul's
Cathedral out of matchsticks in back rooms. With these he
feels at home, because he knows where they're at, and in his
plays he helps us to know too. It is not by chance, I think,
that two of his most wholly satisfactory stage plays, *Mooney
and His Caravans* and *The Mighty Reservoy*, are both extended
duologues, and both show a pair of outcasts – Charley and
Mave, and the ill-assorted couple of men in the water-tower
above the giant reservoir – exploring each other and the

world by coming together in an extreme situation, driven by desperation to some sort of effective contact in shared solitude.

Neither of these plays is by any means flawless: while the obviousness of much of what happens off-stage in *Mooney and His Caravans* is acceptable as all of a piece with the general simplicity of Terson's vision, the melodramatic conclusion of *The Mighty Reservoy* in a turmoil of death and roaring waters could probably be carried off, if at all, only by a more sophisticated writer. Up to that point, though, the developing relationship between the two men, Church and Dron, who are the only two characters, is beautifully managed. Dron is the rough keeper of the new reservoir, and Church an educated visitor, an office worker who feels that at last, up here, he's really getting in touch with the country. The play is hardly more than their relationship, their gradual self-revelation to each other and to us. But we are always conscious of the reservoir itself beneath their feet, a force of nature held in check, perhaps insufficiently, by man: there is, indeed, something rather Laurentian here in Terson's relation of men to natural forces. Eventually, at the end of Act Three, Church disappears into the reservoir and is drowned, but in Act Four he reappears to the drunken Dron with news of a crack in the structure. As the reservoir apparently crashes open Dron 'dies of drink' (how many other modern British playwrights could happily pen that direction?) and in the morning light we recognize that it was all in Dron's head, the reservoir is intact after all.

Of course it is easy to poke fun at certain aspects of these plays, but for all their simplicities, naïveties even, they have real force and power. To my taste they are more personal, and somehow more felt, than the more famous plays in the sequence Terson has written for the National Youth Theatre. These also play with large, simple images, and make the most of their novelty value as really sympathetic, unpatronizing pictures of today's working-class youth seen from the inside, in all their vitality and independence. (This is a lot rarer than one would think, because on the whole, liberal writers seem to find the spectacle of a young working class which is not deserving – let alone poor – does not know its place, and does not have the right reverence for education decidedly disturbing.) But they have the drawback, as far as Terson's special talents are concerned, of being much more about belonging than about exile.

This is partly because of the special circumstances in which they are written. The great advantage of the National Youth Theatre, after all, is its extraordinary feeling of ensemble, and so it is only natural that plays written specifically for them should exploit this quality. *Zigger Zagger* (1967) is essentially the story of two boys from among the crowd: Harry Philton, the dunce at school, hopeless at learning anything, who only comes to life in the grip of football fever, and Zigger Zagger, the leader of the pack. Harry is at most mildly anti-social in his behaviour; but the excitement of the match and the activities of the fans is the only stirring of something real and vital he knows in his life. All the same, he is not unaware of the pressures exerted on him by adult, middle-class society, and in the end, when he has lost his girl Sandra to Vincent, the centre-forward, he decides to jack football in and learn a trade. Zigger jeers at him: the respectable will take him to their bosom, and squeeze the life out of him. But Harry's brother-in-law Les encourages him in his resolve: 'Come on, Harry – life isn't all a football match. *They*'ll find that out . . . Come on, there's no future for you just being in the crowd.'

But Zigger remains the more vivid, memorable character, not so much for what he is as for what he stands for: what everyone in the audience takes away from the play is first and foremost the contagious excitement of the crowds, the well-drilled young company in the stands. And this is perhaps not contrary to Terson's intention. Harry may make the right decision, and certainly he makes the sensible decision. But Terson seems aware that, whatever 'responsible' outsiders may say, by choosing to aim at self-improvement and social acceptance Harry is making himself just a cog in another wheel, and cutting himself off from his one contact with the raw vitality of genuine (if unrespectable) experience. The individual members may drift away, but Zigger is in his way immortal, the crowd goes on for ever, and it is with the crowd chorus that the play ends.

The effect of all this in the theatre is splendid, but *Zigger Zagger* does not finally seem to me very substantial; more a libretto than a play. *The Apprentices* is, coolly considered, a more satisfactory piece, largely because it decides at the start that it is going to be about the decline and fall of Bagley, his gradual isolation in the world to which at the outset he seems to belong completely. Though so to describe it is to beg the issue, or at least to prejudge something which is not so simple as it appears. The story of the play is in a sense the reverse of *Zigger Zagger*. Whereas Harry Philton starts in mild non-conformism and makes his way gradually towards conforming (which may or may not be a good thing), Douglas Bagley starts apparently settled, responsible, all set for a solid, conventional future as an apprentice and then a skilled workman, but gradually moves away from this, refuses to fit in and conform (which equally may or may not be a good thing). He has in him elements of Zigger Zagger, given a local habitation: in the factory yard he is the leader, the great conversationalist, the dominating personality. The picture of the group way of life is less spectacular than in *Zigger Zagger*, but no less impressive. Nothing much happens: the apprentices play around, tease the girls, initiate a newcomer, kick a ball about, go off for a trip in the summer. Bagley gets Betty pregnant and marries her, but still consistently refuses to 'grow up', refuses to fit in and be responsible. All the rest drift off to better jobs or to marry, leaving him, as the Zigger Zaggers of this world are always likely to be left, the world's rejected guest. But for him there is no continuing roar of the crowd to cover over the individual defections. His rebellion, such as it is, is only the smallest possible rebellion – that he will always be the last to clock in. But is what he continues to resist – the nice council house, the steady respectable life – so bad, or is what he wants to keep in its place so good? As in *Zigger Zagger* Terson offers us no easy solutions; and it is notable that he seems to warm progressively to Bagley, and Bagley's predicament, as the passage of time leaves him increasingly isolated, as he, the group leader, ceases to belong and becomes in his turn a sort of exile.

Terson's third play for the National Youth Theatre, *Fuzz*, is the most unashamedly just an outline treatment, a topical, impressionist picture of tearaway youth in conflict with authority, to be filled in by actors and directors with effective action and busy detail. This function it performs excellently, and like its fellows it is finely unpatronizing about the work-ing-class young, but does not get Terson or us – or even the NYT – much forrarder. *Spring-Heeled Jack* (1970) is rather different. This time there is quite a bit of shamelessly old-fashioned plot. Just near Alamein Mansions, a new urban slum, an old tramp woman is found dead, and local hysteria turns it into a murder, the work of the legendary Jack-the-Ripper figure Spring-Heeled Jack. Who is Spring-Heeled Jack? The favourite suspect is Lop Anderson, an old-fashioned teddy boy just out of prison who tries to impress everyone with his bravado but basically just wants to be accepted. Under the leadership of the block's caretaker, a council employee called Badger Openshaw, a sly informer and discreet sadist, the local inhabitants come near to lynching Lop, who is saved in the nick of time only by the intervention of a mild Negro and one-time amateur boxing champion, Everett. There is nothing unexpected about the

story or its working-out, and with a less lively and immaculately organized performance than the National Youth
Theatre gave it the play could be monotonous (the second
half has little even momentary relaxation) and dully
predictable. However, as a starting-point for a typical NYT
production it works perfectly, even if the essential Terson
does not seem to be very seriously involved.

Meanwhile, during the last few years, Terson has been busy
diversifying. While the four NYT plays have turned up
regularly one a year, back in Stoke Terson seems at last to
have got the Vale of Evesham out of his system, and to be
looking round for some other subject. Especially, since
during these four years he has been, for the first time, a full-
time professional writer (a position he is now eager to
relinquish as soon as possible, finding it an intolerable
strain). For a couple of those years he was actually official
resident dramatist at the Victoria Theatre, and then and
since has turned his hand to all sorts of writing jobs, likely
and unlikely, for the company. Among them have been *Sing
an Arful Story*, a largely autobiographical programme of
songs, sketches and stories (1966), put together at short
notice to fill a week's gap in the company's schedule; *The
Knotty* (1966), a musical documentary about the North
Staffordshire Railway, communally elaborated, to which he
contributed research; three Arnold Bennett adaptations,
Jock on the Go, *The Heroism of Thomas Chadwick* (done by the
company for television during their 'exile') and *Clayhanger* (in
collaboration with Joyce Cheeseman); and a children's play,
*The Adventures of Gervase Becket, or The Man Who Changed
Places* (1969), based on the proposition that the challenge to
the contented man is that he should be ready to change places
with anyone he meets who is dissatisfied with his lot.

This period also includes two plays which stand somewhat
aside from anything else Terson has done, *The Ballad of the
Artificial Mash* (1967), and the television play *The Last Train*

through the Harecastle Tunnel (1969). These demonstrate very well both the limitations of his talents and the areas in which he has unfamiliar gifts waiting to be developed. Though the idea of *The Ballad of the Artificial Mash* – a satirical musical about the increasing remoteness of everything we eat from anything nature intended – is appealing, in the event, it seems just about Terson's feeblest work: largely because satire, as John Osborne found out in *The World of Paul Slickey*, requires a special form of sophistication, a degree of intellectual rigour which enables the writer to see his subject with perfect detachment from all possible angles before he selects the precise method by which he will put over his own view.

The Last Train through the Harecastle Tunnel, on the other hand, seems arguably the best of all Terson's plays (interestingly, and perhaps significantly, it is the only one he has written entirely by himself, to be produced almost exactly as it stands). Its form is picaresque, following its railway-obsessed young hero through a succession of strange encounters with all sorts of people – a middle-aged couple in a restaurant car, a retired railwayman who nurtures relics of the past and his flip homosexual son who couldn't care less, a dotty rich man with a whole signal-box reconstructed in his house, an elderly musician who cannot pursue his fascination with railways any more – ranging in their attitudes to his obsession from shared enthusiasm through polite indifference to outright hostility. The hero is, as we might expect, a readymade object of Terson's sympathy, living in his own private world. But what we might not be so prepared for is the crisp exactitude with which he creates the others in a few economical strokes. Earlier, they would probably have remained unseen, as the real world, the people with real power, always do in the Evesham plays. But now he can show us the two sides of a relationship with reality. We are in no doubt where his sympathies lie, but he can see his hero from the other fellow's point of view as well, and in the process he achieves a dramatic complexity which points encouragingly to his possibilities of continuing development as a dramatist.

So do his three last plays at the time of writing. *The 1861 Whitby Lifeboat Disaster* began life as the third section of a 'Whitby Trilogy' of television plays commissioned by the BBC when Terson was living in Whitby in 1968, but it was never produced on television and Terson later rewrote and elaborated it into a full-length stage play. It is founded on a true anecdote. Around the turn of the century a preacher investigating the history of an inmate in a York asylum discovers that his father was one of the lifeboatmen drowned in the famous Whitby disaster. £8000 had been collected by national appeal to care for their widows and orphans, but none of it seems to have reached this particular orphan. Indeed, it turns out that the trustees of the fund decided on reflection that the money, if given to relatives of the victims, might give them ideas above their station, so instead they used it to build a grandiose monument in the local parish church. Most of this emerges in the course of the inquiry which occupies the play's second half, during which the preacher cross-questions survivors in various ways involved with the original disaster and its aftermath. The tale of waste and mismanagement, and even more of the unquestioning acceptance by most of those present of waste and mismanagement as inescapable facts of life, is told with angry directness and unpatronizing compassion which make the play, despite occasional awkwardnesses, a deeply disturbing and at times a touching experience.

In comparison *Prisoners of War*, set in Terson's native Tyneside and first produced at the University Theatre, Newcastle-upon-Tyne, is a minor work, though pleasing; it is semi-autobiographical, a medley of episodes from his childhood during the war, along with some experiences culled from the lives of elders at the same time, and has some quite coincidental points of contact with Peter Nichols's *Forget-Me-Not Lane*, but works at nothing like the same level of intensity. *The Samaritan* (Stoke, 1971), on the other hand, is in every way one of Terson's finest plays. It brings together three disparate characters in one room in London: Godfrey, a full-time Samaritan, Denny, a rather mixed-up character the Samaritans have saved, or half-saved, and the interloper Bob, who calls himself 'a philistine from the rugged north' and sets out, with some at least of the best intentions, to 'bring out' the other two, who have already found a bleak but quite satisfactory *modus vivendi* without him. In neither case do his approaches work: the neurotic Denny retreats into silence faced with so much bonhomie, while Godfrey lets Bob dispense talk and entertainment as long as he likes, only to turn on him in the end and dismiss him as a hollow man – and boring to boot. The play is cunningly constructed to balance our sympathies very precisely: we start by seeing the others through Bob's eyes, and so willy-nilly being on his side, and then gradually Terson lets us see more and more clearly how Bob seems to them. All three characters are beautifully drawn, but especially Bob, with his forlorn fantasy of return to his lost working-class roots, and the melodrama and sentimentality which might be inherent in the subject are avoided by being totally disregarded, even as remote possibilities.

No doubt Terson will continue to develop, as he will continue to write plays. Despite his feeling that it is time to slow down his output a bit, and despite his decision to withdraw from being a full-time writer, it is clear that the urge to write is with him obsessive. As he says himself,

'Once I went into the room of an old fellow, well in his eighties, in Stoke. And the whole place was full of elaborate fretwork models of famous buildings of the world, cut and shaped and assembled from thousands of tiny pieces of wood, matchsticks and the like. And I thought to myself, how extraordinary to devote years of your life to an obsession like that, knowing it doesn't mean a thing to anyone but you. And then I thought, but my writing is like that. I'm just lucky that because my plays are produced, they do have a chance to mean something to someone else after all. And for that at least I am grateful.'

Joe Orton

In all the history of the New Drama in Britain there is no career more spectacular, and alas none briefer, than that of Joe Orton. Between his first play, *The Ruffian on the Stair*, produced on the Third Programme in 1964, and his sudden death in 1967, he wrote three full-length stage plays and three television plays, plus an original film script (which has not yet reached production) and various other oddments, including presumably the sketch about an incestuous county family which surfaced in the London version of *Oh! Calcutta!* (1970). But even within this brief period he had not only written two of the new dramatists' biggest commercial successes, *Entertaining Mr Sloane* and *Loot*, but had developed his own unmistakable vision of the world and his own tone of voice as a dramatist – to such an extent that ever after one finds oneself reading actual news stories in terms of a Joe Orton script.

The key to Orton's dramatic world is to be found in the strange relationship between the happenings of his plays and the manner in which the characters speak of them. The happenings may be as outrageous as you like in terms of morality, accepted convention or whatever, but the primness and propriety of what is said hardly ever breaks down. And the gift of Orton's characters for intricate and inventive euphemism, so far from toning down the outrageousness of their actions and ideas, only places it in even stronger relief. Orton was, perhaps first and foremost, a master of verbal style – or of his own particular verbal style. And even during his short public career his mastery of that style may be observed increasing and refining itself.

It is very instructive, for example, to compare the original text of *The Ruffian on the Stair*, as published in the BBC volume *New Radio Drama*, with the revised version staged at the Royal Court only two years later in the double bill *Crimes of Passion*. Everywhere the dialogue is cut and rephrased with unerring precision to bring out the particular Orton flavour, already present in the original but muted and indecisive. For example, when the mysterious young man Wilson comes to the door inexplicably demanding a room for rent, the dialogue in the original went:

WILSON. I've come about the room.
JOYCE. What room?
WILSON. Didn't you advertise? In the shop down the road?
JOYCE. Who sent you?
WILSON. I saw the card in the window.
JOYCE. You must have made a mistake.
WILSON. Didn't you advertise? I've got the wrong address?
JOYCE. We've no room.
  Pause
WILSON. I'm not a Jew. (*Pause.*) I'm not coloured.
JOYCE. I can see that.
WILSON. I was brought up in the Home Counties. My father was foreign. He wasn't native to this country. We'd better get that straight. He came from abroad. (*Pause.*) Is this the room?

In the second version this whole passage is transformed into:

WILSON (*smiling*). I've come about the room.
JOYCE. I'm afraid there's been a mistake. I've nothing to do with allotting rooms. Make your inquiries elsewhere.
WILSON. I'm not coloured. I was brought up in the Home Counties.
JOYCE. That doesn't ring a bell with me, I'm afraid.
WILSON. Is that the room?

There is obviously an influence here, I think: that of Pinter. Indeed the initial situation of the play makes this almost inevitable. But its later developments take it off in a quite un-Pinterish direction, and show Orton elaborating and defining his own attitudes as well as his dramatic method. He is, for example, much more concerned than Pinter with the elaboration of plot, obsessively detailed and precise plot. Like the highly formal language his characters speak, the intricate plots through which they are manœuvred create a critical distance between play and spectator. One is always aware in Orton that he is using a convention to make his points, even though he himself always insisted that in a very important sense his plays are realistic (the sense, as I understand it, that they embody his observations of what happens within society in the real world and are written in a style which seems to him perfectly natural, however odd it may seem to anyone else). It is a convention suggestive at once of the two surviving genres of truly popular theatre, farce and the whodunnit, both of which require intricate plot and simplified, or at any rate very simple, characterization. It is obviously significant that in later plays he makes the connection explicit: *Loot* is on one level both a whodunnit and a parody of a whodunnit; *What the Butler Saw* is both a farce and a parody of a farce.

Nearly all these elements are present, at least embryonically, in *The Ruffian on the Stair*. Before he wrote it, according to his own account, he had failed his examinations (in Leicester, where he was born in 1933), been fired from several jobs for incompetence, studied two years at RADA and acted in rep for four months, married, divorced (these, it seems, were apocryphal), been arrested for larceny and put in prison for six months, and written one playlet, a dialogue between a very old man dying in hospital and his seventy-year-old daughter, which had attracted friendly if hardly enthusiastic attention from the BBC and the Royal Court. He had also, during his time at RADA, met another actor manqué and would-be writer, Kenneth Halliwell, set up house with him, and written in collaboration with him various extravagant pieces of fiction, all unpublished, with such titles as *The Last Days of Sodom* and *Priapus in the Shrubbery*. The prison sentence both he and Halliwell served was for stealing and defacing library books – in just the same way that Max Beerbohm fancifully reworked the texts and illustrations of many books, only with the vital distinction that he at least owned the books in question. The ménage with Halliwell survived, despite ups and downs, until in a jealous fury one night in August 1967 Halliwell beat out Orton's brains then killed himself with an overdose of pills.

The Ruffian on the Stair, which Orton wrote on leaving prison, was his first work to be accepted (for radio production), though it did not actually go out until after the first critical success of *Entertaining Mr Sloane*. It starts from the Pinterish situation of a middle-aged woman living a life of apparent respectability (even if the man she is living with is not her husband and she was admittedly on the game before she took up with him) who is suddenly confronted by a young man at the door determined to move in and quite impervious to any arguments which deny Joyce's responsibility for 'allotting rooms'. But even before this the clues have been dropped which point to the eventual course of the action. Mike, Joyce's man, has admitted to running a van, and Joyce has been talking about a mysterious accident involving a tattooed man run down by a van. And now it gradually emerges that Wilson, the intruder, is not there by chance or even for one of those reasons, like that for the arrival of Goldberg and McCann in *The Birthday Party*, which tease us and work on us by their very lack of definition. Eventually the hints are taken up and the secret motives revealed, in the best well-made-play tradition: the tattooed man, run down by Mike, was Wilson's brother, loved with more than brotherly devotion, and Wilson has a plan for revenge, which will incidentally serve his own secondary purpose, suicide. He sets up the situation between himself and Joyce in such a way that Mike will kill him from jealousy and then have to answer for the second killing in place of the first.

It is a very curious mixture: an intricate 'revenger's tragedy' compressed into one act and played as farce. Even more curious is that, although it was only a first play, Orton manages to bring it off – even in the first, more tentative version. Obviously he was talented, but from this play alone one would be hard put to it to decide whether he was extraordinarily sophisticated technically or possessed of a happy innocence which enabled him to walk his particular dramatic tightrope with the certainty of a sleepwalker. Even after five more plays I am still not sure what the answer to that one should be. But at least in *Entertaining Mr Sloane*, *Loot*, and *The Erpingham Camp*, he shows every sign of knowing precisely what he is doing, at every level on which the plays work, so I suppose the happy innocent view of his talent will not really hold water.

All the same, it is difficult not to wonder whether he was fully aware of his own singularity. I am inclined to believe him when he said that as far as he was concerned his dialogue seemed perfectly realistic, naturalistic even. The other work of literature which most immediately springs to mind in connection with *Entertaining Mr Sloane* is Daisy Ashford's *The Young Visiters*, a Victorian child's picture of life among the high and mighty in which language is very seriously, but rather insecurely, on its grandest best behaviour. I am sure Orton knew perfectly well that his dialogue was funny, but I am not entirely convinced that he knew precisely how and why it was.

What is beautifully kept up in *Mr Sloane*, rather less so in his other plays, is the almost surrealistic dislocation between the most extraordinary and improper happenings and the unruffled propriety of the characters' conversation. The two elements are held in perfect balance. On the one hand the exemplary tale of the entertaining Mr Sloane, magnetic but dangerous, who has already killed one man and in the course of the play will kill another, being caught in his own trap, the biter bit; and on the other the gradual revelation that the respectable-looking suburban household of middle-aged woman, doddering father and regularly visiting businessman brother into which he comes, so sure of himself, is, for all its façade of respectability, its refined speech and genteel manners, far more outrageous, far more dangerous, than anything Mr Sloane has in his silly little head.

The unrolling of the plot is timed with extraordinary skill and assurance, especially considering that this was Orton's first full-length play. The Kemp family, with their solitary house in the middle of a rubbish dump, consists of Kath, a superannuated Baby Doll whose often expressed desire to be motherly demonstrates itself chiefly in her habit of wandering round 'in the rude' under her flimsy dress, and virtually raping her lodger on his first night there; Ed, a stolid businessman homosexual with a taste for body-builders who drops in from time to time; and Dadda, a nasty-tempered old man who has not spoken to Ed for twenty years, ever since he found him 'committing some kind of felony in the bedroom'. Into this cosy little den of suburban iniquity wanders the smooth-skinned, fair-haired Mr Sloane, a grubby suburban Adonis. Kath, having lured Sloane in, assumes automatically that he is panting with desire for her, and Sloane is by no means loth to take advantage of a cushy situation. Ed objects, but when he sees Sloane, he rapidly changes his tune and starts instead to give Sloane big-brotherly advice about the dangers of a healthy lad tangling with those nasty creatures, women.

But Sloane is clearly a murderer (Dadda keeps rumbling on about his suspicions), on the loose and very possibly psychopathic. We might be in for another *Night Must Fall*, with the family welcoming into their bosom decidedly more than they bargained for. But not a bit of it; in the event it proves to be the murderer who is no match for them; he is pettish, childish, and does not know what he wants beyond the immediate requisites of a life of comfort, inactivity, and as far as possible luxury; Kath and Ed, on the other hand, know exactly what they want, and know well enough how to get it. In a word, they want him. They are ready to make his cage reasonably gilded, to treat their pet well, but they will not stand any signs of independence from him, and regard his murder of their old father quite blandly ('Well, it's been a pleasant morning,' remarks Ed casually when it's all over) as a good weapon to use against him in keeping him under control. What looked like being a story of a cuckoo in the nest has turned, almost before we know what is happening, into another tale of the spider and the fly.

The play is a comedy of language, but it is also a comedy of manners: the humour derives as much from gradual revelation of character as from the manipulation of spoken words. And formally it is immaculately managed: the clue to its structure is in the title, the meaning of which inexorably shifts in the course of the play from providing entertainment for Mr Sloane to using Mr Sloane as an occasion of entertainment. And the conclusion, in which Mr Sloane finds himself being divided cheerfully between his voracious (and now pregnant) hostess and her equally voracious brother for alternate six-month periods is not only eminently satisfactory as a resolution in human terms, but formally as unarguably final as the three chimes of the bell at the end of Stravinsky's *Les Noces*.

Loot (1965), in comparison, is not quite so satisfactory. Partly, I think, this is because the balance has shifted slightly in the direction of farce, and it seems to me that the degree of human believability accorded the characters in *The Ruffian on the Stair* and *Entertaining Mr Sloane* is important to the proper functioning of Orton's drama: without that, it tends over too far towards abstraction, and *Loot*, for all its delights, is a little arid, a play about plays and play conventions rather than a play which is, however remotely, about (if you will pardon the word) life.

The starting-point is a parody of the conventional thriller/ whodunnit. A corpse is present, lying in state and murdered, as it transpires, by one of the other characters, a nurse who, it also transpires, has previously made a career out of mass-murdering patients, employers and husbands. Meanwhile, Hal McLeavy, the son of the house, sublimely unaware of the precise details of his mother's end, not to mention the present designs Nurse Fay has on his newly widowed father, has got involved with a friend (or rather-more-than-friend) in a bank robbery and is now called on to conceal the loot (in the coffin – where else?). Enter Inspector Truscott of the Yard, disguised as a man from the Water Board who, he points out whenever his authority is questioned, have rights of entry more complete and unequivocal than any the police can claim. Fay rapidly discovers what the young men are up to (owing to Hal's unfortunate inability to tell a lie), and assists them, at a price. All seems fated when the hearse taking the coffin for burial is involved in a crash, but the charred coffin is returned with money intact. Meanwhile Truscott is biding his time before arresting Fay for murder. She confesses in a properly businesslike fashion: 'Very good,' observes Truscott admiringly: 'Your style is simple and direct. It's a theme which less skilfully handled could've given offence.' But then, owing to the disappearance of the deceased's viscera (along with much else), Truscott has no evidence on which to make the arrest. However, the provenance of a mysterious glass eye he has found lying around bothers Truscott, and he wants to see the body of Mrs McLeavy. Everyone by now has some reason for trying to prevent him, but in the general dazzle of changing stories, lightning reversals, corpse and money in and out of the coffin with the speed of a jack-in-the-box, he happens upon the money, which is now reposing in the casket intended for the missing viscera. And so we are led up to a sublimely immoral, properly improper conclusion in which they all, except the unfortunate McLeavy, carried protesting off to prison, agree to share out the money and go their own ways towards . . .

Well, towards what? One has no illusion that the characters have any existence at all outside the confines of what we actually see and hear, or will go on existing after the play is done. Of course this is only an illusion (we all know the proper answer to 'How many children had Lady Macbeth?' or 'What crime did Stanley commit to be treated the way he is in *The Birthday Party?*'), but it is an illusion which may well be rather important in the life of a play. In *Loot* Orton makes no bones about treating his characters as puppets, and though the play has some very funny lines, it lacks the extra dimension *Mr Sloane* has simply because we relate the words and actions of its characters to some recognizable external reality.

I think *Loot* still works, because the elements of parody are effective enough in themselves, and some of the ideas conveyed in what is actually said (as apart from any relation the lines may have to the character of those speaking them) are pleasingly outrageous enough to keep us agreeably amused throughout an evening in the theatre. But the play lacks the density and resonance of *Entertaining Mr Sloane*, and so does tend to fade rather rapidly from the memory. Nor is its leading idea, the attack on religious hypocrisy (or rather Orton's cool observation of the discrepancy between the formal practice of religion and the way those practising it actually behave in their everyday lives), though much has been made of its significance by some critics, really effectively put over, precisely because Orton's contracting-out of human drama more or less forbids us to apply what he is saying in the real world outside the confines of his stage.

The Erpingham Camp (1966) is considerably more effective

in this respect, because its leading idea – of a holiday camp as a sort of voluntary concentration camp – though not entirely novel, has enough recognizable truth in it, enough relation to the known traits of sufficiently believable human beings, to produce resonances in our minds beyond the confines of what we see before us immediately on the television screen (where it started life) or the stage (where it arrived a year later in double harness with *The Ruffian on the Stair*). The play is skilfully constructed in a single crescendo of action. At the start, Erpingham is awaiting the arrival of a new entertainments organizer at his holiday camp (almost as scarifying in its way as Mooney's in Peter Terson's *Mooney and his Caravans*), and parrying the urgent requests of Redcoat Riley to be given the job. When Riley returns with the news that the new arrival has promptly been taken seriously ill, and is followed by the Padre to say that he is dead, Erpingham has little alternative but to put Riley in charge, just for that night. Riley starts out well enough, but he has no notion how to keep the customers happy. Almost at once he is in trouble when he recruits two gormless couples we have already met, the wives, Lou and Eileen, for a screaming competition, the husbands, Kenny and Ted, respectively to be the week's Tarzan in a leopard skin and to strip in order to dance a can-can. From then on what started as a jolly evening's entertainment gets hopelessly out of hand and ends in a bacchic rout with the camp in flames, several dead (including Erpingham himself) and honour not satisfied until the Padre takes over and organizes a memorial service over the mangled remains of Erpingham.

The play has many nice ruthless jokes in Orton's best fantastic vein, such as Erpingham's cheery loudspeaker announcement near the beginning that 'Our disability bonus was won by Mr Laurie Russel of Market Harborough. Both Laurie's legs were certified "absolutely useless" by our Resident Medical Officer. Yet he performed the Twist and

the Bossa Nova to the tune specified on the entrance form'
(at which Ted practically observes 'He fell over though.
Twice'). Orton's use of language here is also at his most
masterly: the constantly repeated formulas culled from
sentimental journalism ('We were refused permission to wed.
We defied the ban on our love') serve not only to amuse in
themselves, but to tell us something about the characters who
use them, to limit and direct our response to them (rather
than being, as in *Loot*, a simple inclusive formula, a convention which all observe). Also, we see the convention breaking
down under the impact of experience, so that when Kenny,
the love-ban husband, suddenly squares up to Erpingham
with the cry 'You'll pay for this, you ignorant fucker!', the
effect is quite as cataclysmic as that of any of the physical
violence depicted.

The Good and Faithful Servant (1967), Orton's second television play and the last work to be produced during his
lifetime, takes off in a completely different direction, and
shows a remarkable extension of his range. It is a sad,
ruthless picture of an old man's decline and death after his
retirement from a vast, faceless firm in which he has spent
fifty years of his life and yet where no one remembers him or,
after a few months, even knows his name. On the day of his
retirement he discovers by chance that the old char is his
long-lost love, that as a result of their brief encounter she had
twins, and that both were later killed in Italy. But all that is
long past and it's too late to do anything now, except to marry
the char and meet a surviving grandson. Ray does in fact
enter George's life, but is little consolation, what with his
layabout habits and his entanglement with Debbie at the
works, whom he has thoughtlessly impregnated. A visit to
the firm's social club, where everyone, badgered and bullied
by the personnel officer, agrees to fit in even though no one
knows anyone else and they all seem to hate it, is disastrous.
As George dies, Ray's reform is announced together with his

decision to marry Debbie and settle down – no doubt to fifty years of everything that killed George.

Some of the play is very funny, and it has lines in Orton's best manner, but for once the style never seems in danger of taking over control; it is kept firmly in its place. And despite the harsh irony of the play, with its merciless picture of the not ill-intentioned but entirely overbearing and insensitive Mrs Vealfoy, who nearly plagues the life out of poor George, a surprising amount of compassion and human warmth – not qualities we would normally associate with Orton – comes through. Maybe this was a fluke, a sport in Orton's garden of effects; but it is tempting to suggest that here he came as near as anywhere to wearing his heart on his sleeve.

It is, of course, quite as pointless to speculate on what Orton would have done next had he lived (instead of being murdered in circumstances which might have come from one of his own plays) as it is to wonder what happens next to any of the characters in his plays. All the same, it is inevitable. I do not myself believe that the posthumous production of his television play *Funeral Games* and his stage play *What the Butler Saw* did any service to his memory. Both give the impression of being, at best, rough drafts which he would surely have changed, enriched, refined, or perhaps even have chucked away altogether if he had been spared. *Funeral Games* carries the method of *Loot* further: it was accepted by many critics at the time of its production as being 'bold', but the boldness is mainly a matter of form.

The action takes place in a never-never land where the newsworthy leader of a new sect considers taking a journalist to court for daring to suggest that he did not in fact (as he is generally credited with doing) murder his wife. Actually he has thought of doing so, eager to get her out of the way and ensnare a rich benefactress, but on reflection has left her living with a defrocked cleric and simply let everyone assume she is dead. Unfortunately the defrocked cleric *has* murdered *his* wife, who proves to have been the bishop's wife's best friend, but at least the body comes in useful for supplying necessary evidence of the bishop's guilt to still the doubts of the public. In the circumstances it is hard to relate characters or events to any external reality, and therefore to any existing code or convention of morality, propriety and what-have-you. But if this is a fantasy world where anything goes, then how can you hope to bring off effects which depend on a sense of outrage at the breaking of taboos? Shock cannot exist without at least some partial, provisional sense of belief. It must also be said that some of the plotting is so slipshod that it could not get by even in high tragedy, let alone that most logical of all forms, low farce.

What the Butler Saw is in almost exactly the same situation. It tries to work like *Loot*, only this time guying the conventions of farce instead of the whodunnit. But to burlesque something which depends from the beginning on its qualities of burlesque is almost a logical impossibility: if you parody a parody where do you end up, if not back where you started? True, the vehicle of farce could be used to convey something which farce is not normally required to convey, but that does not seem to be seriously in question here: much of the play merely takes up conventions which those using them have always known to be absurd, delighted in for their very absurdity, and draws our attention, unsurprisingly, to the fact that they are absurd. The answer to the playwright can only be: Yes, but so what? What then? Is the play about anything beyond the conventions of play-writing (or a certain kind of play-writing)?

What the Butler Saw isn't – or anyway, in so far as we can guess at what it is meant to be about, it does not manage actually to express it. The play's epigraph is 'Surely we're all mad people, and they whom we think are, are not', which suggests that the complete insanity of everyone on stage is deliberate, and is intended to make some point about the world at large. But if so there is at least a bad technical error involved: to make comedy out of the extraordinary, a play needs a norm, and farce above all needs its straight man. So much depends on context: if there is no inherent reason why anyone should not come on and say or do anything, then we shall rapidly cease to be surprised and outraged (or even amused) by anything they say or do. The play soon becomes reduced to a succession of lines and happenings in a total vacuum. And anything for a laugh is always the shakiest standard a dramatist can possibly set himself.

What the Butler Saw, in the version produced in London, comes out very much like that. (A heavily edited version produced off Broadway has apparently proved more successful.) A psychiatrist gets involved in an endless series of complicated misunderstandings arising from his initial frantic attempts to disguise from his wife and another visiting psychiatrist a minor and anyway abortive peccadillo with a new secretary, semi-nude, in his consulting-room. Fair enough: many a successful farce has been built on less. But for us to be amused by it we have to have some feeling of a rigid, unbreakable code of convention (idiotically so, perhaps) governing what the characters may, or are assumed to be able to, do. Every such convention and assumption is methodically demolished in this case. We soon learn that the relationship between the psychiatrist and his wife is one of naked hostility: he married her for her money and then found out she hadn't any, he has tried to murder her, and she, for her part, is an avowed nymphomaniac belonging to a lesbian club and, we may suppose, as sophisticated as possible in sexual matters. Why then should either he or she be supposed to care what he is doing with his secretary?

Similarly with the visiting psychiatrist who arbitrarily takes over the hero's consulting-room: he assumes that the normal relationship between doctor and secretary is that of lovers, which gives us one funny line but makes nonsense of his unwilling host's elaborate subterfuges. For they can be funny only if related to a recognizable context of clear-cut theoretical morality such as Orton goes out of his way to demolish in nearly every line he writes. And if it is the conventions themselves Orton is making fun of, then he has got his and our lines inextricably crossed by trying to do so within a form which depends on convention for its essential structure and indeed its very existence. Thus undermined, the play's later complications of plot, involving a pageboy who is blackmailing the psychiatrist's wife, a policeman who comes to arrest the pageboy for seducing a whole school dormitory, an exchange of clothes between pageboy and secretary, and an apparent series of revelations which prove that the sane are mad and nobody is who he appears to be anyway, become increasingly spiritless and mechanical, to the point where even dutiful laughter stops altogether.

It is clearly unfair to go into such detail taking apart a play which comes to us in what we may presume to be an extremely provisional form. It is only because what seem to me very exaggerated claims for it as Orton's best play, a subtle and profound moral statement, the most glittering artificial comedy in English since Congreve and so on have been made that I bother to do so. For it seems to me that though Orton's best work is *Entertaining Mr Sloane*, he went on developing his gifts and revealing new aspects of them in everything which was performed during his lifetime, and it is only in the light of the two posthumously produced plays that one begins to question the strength and durability of his talent. That his talent was genuine and extraordinary I have no doubt. The sudden crop of imitators after his first successes bears witness at least to the marked individuality of his writing, while the inability of any of the writers in the 'school of Orton' (best of them probably Simon Gray in *Wise Child* and *Dutch Uncle*) to come anywhere near the quality of the original demonstrates that even if his mannerisms were easy to mimic Orton was, finally, inimitable. And in *Entertaining Mr Sloane* he managed, at the very lowest estimate, to write the first solid, well-managed commercial play which belonged, specifically and unmistakably, to the post-Osborne era.

I think there is more to the play, and to Orton, than that. It is remarkable, for example, that though they seem to start from the material of camp fantasy, Orton's plays manage completely to transform that material into a serious vision of life, which, however, eccentric – and however comic in its chosen forms of expression – carries complete conviction as something felt, something true. (It was not for nothing that Orton said, commenting on the possibility of an American production for *Loot*, 'I don't want there to be anything queer or camp or odd about the relationship of Hal and Dennis. Americans see homosexuality in terms of fag and drag. This isn't my vision of the universal brotherhood . . . I won't have the Great American Queen brought into it.') But even on the humble level of providing commercial entertainment in the modern manner, what he did was unique, in its own way epoch-making, and surely entitles him to at least a footnote in even the severest histories of drama in our time.

David Storey

From a quick glance at the external facts, you might suppose that David Storey's career as a writer was simple and clear-cut in its shape, if intriguingly obscure in its motivation. First, three successful novels, appearing at respectably regular intervals. Then, four plays, also nicely spaced out over four years. The inference seems to be obvious: a case of mistaken vocation, or rather, given the excellence of the novels, a case of changed vocation, like that of John Mortimer, who has recorded that his first attempt to write a play, after six novels, was like coming home, finding the ideal medium which thereafter removed all desire in him to write novels ever again.

But this first impression, like many first impressions, would be wrong in David Storey's case. To begin with, it does not fit the facts. His first play, *The Restoration of Arnold Middleton*, though not produced until 1967, was actually written around 1959, more or less between his first novel, *This Sporting Life*, and his second, *Flight into Camden*. At this time, discouraged by his failure to find a publisher for *This Sporting Life*, even after several rewrites, he was beginning to wonder whether he was really a novelist at all, whether he might not after all be a dramatist instead. So, since he was then teaching, he devoted a few days off to writing a play about a teacher who goes mad and kills himself (it was then called *To Die with the Philistines*). The immediate result was no more encouraging: a few faint displays of interest led to nothing and for four years or so it languished on agents' shelves. Storey went back to novel-writing, wrote *Flight into Camden* and, when *This Sporting Life* was finally published in 1960, became a name to conjure with. He might have stuck with novel-writing and not given a further thought to the theatre – he admits to not being at all interested in the theatre and rarely going – if Lindsay Anderson had not brought his thoughts back to drama at a time when he was feeling some concern and dissatisfaction over critical responses to his first two novels. The occasion was the making of Lindsay Anderson's film based on *This Sporting Life* in 1963 (which Storey scripted), and an inquiry from Anderson about whether he had ever written or thought of writing a play. This reminded him of *The Restoration of Arnold Middleton*, which he dusted off and extensively revised for an abortive production at the Royal Court in 1964.

The readiness to do this, and the nature of the revisions, reflect some of Storey's unhappiness with the reception of his first two novels. *This Sporting Life*, in particular, had, inexplicably as one now looks at it, been taken as a straight-forward realistic picture of life in the North and the rise and fall of a Rugby League footballer, part of a new wave of documentary fiction the critics were then busy enthusing over. *Flight into Camden*, a first-person novel about a woman who cannot cope with the world about her, was mostly found just mystifying. Storey felt the reception of both of them badly missed the point of his intentions, which had more to do with the relation of the inner life to the outer life (the central character of each novel can manage one but not the other) than with documentary realism, so he set about completing *Radcliffe*, and revising *Arnold Middleton*, in some determination that this time round he would direct his audience's attention very specifically to what he wanted them to see. He says now that he thinks this was a mistake, and the side effects of the reaction are what spoil the book and to a lesser extent the play for him in retrospect.

'You see, I wrote the book starting from about chapter five, then went back and wrote the first chapters – which didn't fit the rest at all! – and put in linking passages to impose on it a sort of overall pattern of significance, the significance I then saw in what I had written, according to which the two principal characters are facets of the same thing, body and mind, outer and inner life, brought together. The result was that *Radcliffe* is scattered with great big notices saying "Pay attention now, this is significant", and I think that spoils the book. I did a bit the same with the play. It was at this point that the suit of armour Arnold plays about with first appeared. I don't know that that was an improvement; I think it's just that bit too much pushing something right under people's noses. And of course I changed the ending so that he lived. Again, I don't know if that was right: it might have been better to follow out the logic of the story, as I did at first. But it was honest in another way, because I was I suppose in a rather despairing state myself when I first wrote the play, and when I came to revise I said to myself, but I'm still alive, and working, so I must see some sort of possibility of going on and getting somewhere, so in a certain sense the original ending was not really "true" either.'

Also, Storey admits that, working on the film of *This Sporting Life*, he appreciated fully for the first time the advantages of the dramatic media for directing an audience's responses through angling and selection, in a way which is much more difficult in the more expansive medium of the novel.

'Writing a novel is like launching an unmanned ship. You may direct it in a certain direction, but thereafter you have no further control over it, it's out of your hands. A play is like a properly crewed ship: you can modify from moment to moment, take account of the climate of feeling at any particular performance, test out ideas and if they don't work as you want them to, change them.'

These advantages were not immediately demonstrated, though, since plans for production had to be put aside, and *The Restoration of Arnold Middleton* did not finally appear on stage until 1967.

It was the production of the play which really set Storey off again on play-writing. He had found himself in difficulties with his new novel, and suddenly his energies, blocked in that direction, poured out in five or six plays, all written very quickly, often in only two or three days each. Both *In Celebration* and *The Contractor* date from this outburst of activity; since, he has written three or four more plays, and he keeps plugging away at that novel; or rather, those novels, since he has written, in whole or in part, several since *Radcliffe* which do not satisfy him, one of them running to 350,000 words, which as he says is a lot of work just to throw away. But then he seems to feel genuine mystification about all the functionings of his creative processes: he writes first, in longhand, then examines what he has written as he types it out, and often finds that his expectations are completely confounded: something he thought was going splendidly while he was writing it seems completely dead on the page, something which he really didn't like at all at the time somehow works. For example, of his fourth produced play, *Home*, he wrote two versions, or two different plays with the same title and idea ('You remember the white table at the end of *The Contractor*? Well, this play starts from there, from the image of that white table . . .'), one of which he thought was going swimmingly and then hated when he came to type it, the other he hated while writing it and then found to his pleasure and surprise that it worked.

Strange, this erratic and unpredictable way of writing, these extremes of reaction to the completed texts, given that in many respects Storey's plays seem rather anachronistically balanced, direct and realistic, beautifully shaped and with a meticulous notation of everyday speech. So much so that critics have started bandying the name of Chekhov about in their vicinity, and commenting on how well-made and – what was until very recently the last word in polite damnation – 'well-written' they are. But Storey explains the criteria by which he judges the success or failure of his writings, whether they work for him or not, very convincingly.

'It seems to me that if, on reading something through, I know completely what it is about, then it is dead. It is when I feel that I don't really know what it is about that it lives – it lives for me almost in the measure that it escapes and refuses definition. The rejected *Home* I understood completely, so it had the deadness of a demonstration; the other one, the produced version, rather mystified me, but it had taken on an independent life of its own.

'It is for this reason that I find *The Contractor* one of the most satisfying things I've written. Each time I see it in a different light. In this revival [when the play transferred to the West End] I see it more and more as being about – or somehow related to – the decline and fading-away of a capitalist society. Or I have seen it as a metaphor for artistic creation; all the labour of putting up this tent, and when it's there, what good is it? What is it there for? And I get letters from people who ask me does it mean this, and does it mean that, and I often see some justice in their suggestions. And still the play is not confined to any one of these definitions; it contains the possibility of them, but it still continues to make sense – and complete sense – as the story of these men who put up this tent, and that's that. I think it's very important for me to leave all the options open . . .'

It is precisely this quality – the teasing and elusive feeling that the plays have a sort of weight and density which one cannot logically justify – which makes David Storey's plays (and for that matter his novels) so distinctive in the contemporary British scene. One would guess, I think, that though the plays have an extraordinary and unerring instinct for what works in the theatre, they were written by someone with no passionate interest in the theatre or close involvement in the latest movements, the approved positions for a modern playwright. A lot of their material is clearly autobiographical – not so much, presumably, in the details of plot, character and situation, but in the backgrounds and ways of life evoked: Storey, born in 1933, comes from the North of *In Celebration*, has been, like the hero of *This Sporting Life*, a professional footballer and, like the hero of *Arnold Middleton*, a teacher, has worked in a tent-erecting firm such as provides the background for *Radcliffe* and *The Contractor*. The experiences give immediacy and body to his works; but finally any documentary interest is strictly coincidental. They are so compelling because of the intensity with which they summon up one man's private vision of the world.

This is already evident in *The Restoration of Arnold Middleton*, which, despite its author's reservations, strikes me as a remarkably successful play, keeping its knife-edge balance between reality and fantasy with stunning professional aplomb. Its major problem for the writer is that its hero is going mad, and the mad on stage, though apparently making everything easy by permitting any vagary of behaviour, actually make coherent drama considerably more difficult. Storey solves the problem very neatly, by not allowing us to realize for sure that Arnold is going mad until he is actually on the point of being restored. He is eccentric, admittedly, but then characters who cultivate eccentricities as a defence against the world are by no means unfamiliar in recent English writing, especially when they are schoolteachers. It is tempting to say that Arnold behaves like Lucky Jim for Jimmy Porterish reasons. The surface is all schoolboyish japes, tall stories about his trying to sneak an oversized suit of armour into school under the headmaster's nose, and little academic jokes with other members of the staff. But they arise, not from Lucky Jim's brainless philistinism, but from a real anguish with the world for not being what he wants it to be. He looks for strength, for majesty; he asks too much of people, and they fail him. So he seeks refuge in a shell of his own choosing, an obsessive barrage of music-hall comedy and nursery rhyme nonsense through which anyone hoping to penetrate to his soft centre and make him, just for once, react must try, usually in vain, to pierce.

Like old Mrs Phineus in Arden's biting comedy *The Happy Haven*, he would like to say,

> Leave me be, but don't leave me alone,
> That's what I want. I'm a big round stone
> Sitting in the middle of a thunderstorm.

But his wife is too inclined to leave him alone, and not inclined enough to leave him be. And meanwhile, behind the façade, the man is crumbling; he must break down before he can be built up again. A lot in the early scenes is very funny, and though we are conscious of something else working away underneath, it is very difficult to put a finger on exactly what it is. Then comes the scene in which Arnold, having actually gone mad, passes his crisis and begins his restoration. After what has gone before, it is a remarkably daring piece of dramaturgy, brilliantly brought off: the suit of armour, subject of a joke before, is now palpably present on stage. Arnold's wife cannot take any more and is determined to hit back, his mother-in-law is upstairs in a state of collapse, and he is left alone, addressing the armour in a long, loosely versified monologue about his parents' teachings in his childhood:

> . . . remember, even if the means are insufficient, rather
> Than die in pieces subside by preference as a whole,
> For disintegration is inimical to the soul
> Which seeks the opportunity or the chances
> To die in the circumstances
> Of a prince, a saviour, or a messiah . . .

The process thus begun is well on the way by the next, final scene: his long-resident mother-in-law is at last leaving, and Arnold feels – it is only 'an assumption based on a generality of feeling' – that he can come out, is coming out. It is an enormous dramatic leap, and yet so true is the feeling, so solid the characterization, that one believes, and it works. But one could be forgiven for wondering, seeing that this is, after all, a first play, if this success was just a happy accident, one of those things a beginner can occasionally bring off because he is ready blithely to rush in where old pros, with reason, fear to tread.

In Celebration (1969) soon put paid to any such speculation. It is another study of the mind at the end of its tether, or nearly – for as Storey seems to have decided in his revisions of *Arnold Middleton*, the extraordinary thing about the human animal is his ability to keep going, even when everything seems impossible. The occasion is the fortieth wedding anniversary of the Shaws, an old coal-miner and his wife, which brings their three surviving sons, Andrew, Colin and Steven, home together again for one night. Gradually we see that all three of them, despite their varying degrees of success in the outside world, have all been psychologically crippled by their background and upbringing, and particularly it seems by the legacy of guilt from the death in childhood of an earlier-born brother, a brother conceived out of wedlock whose imminent arrival compelled their mother to marry beneath her and set up obscure chain reactions which are still reverberating in the adult lives of the whole family.

At least, this is the interpretation put upon things by Andrew, the most dynamic and, in worldly terms, the least successful of them. He still hugs to him his capacity for suffering, and his role in the family reunion turns out to be largely that of *agent provocateur*, forcing the others to look at themselves and one another again in the light of his own bitter logic, to feel something, if they still can, instead of atrophying because of their unwillingness to face any kind of emotional reality, accept any kind of emotional challenge, any more. He has recently taken an important step in his life by walking out of his job as a solicitor to become a painter; his quieter brother Steven has decided not to finish a book he was working on for some years on the subject of modern society. The third brother, Colin, is the only one who seems secure and externally successful; he is saner and more sensible than the others, but this seems to be the main charge against him – as far as Andrew is concerned, this is the measure of his sell-out. But even more important than getting back at Colin is getting back at the mother, who is felt in some obscure way to be responsible for all their spiritual ills.

The play is seemingly loose and discursive, but essentially it is very tightly knit, with no word or gesture left which could be taken away without damaging the delicate organization of the whole, the gradual stripping of layer after layer from the characters until they all seem to be stripped spiritually naked. (In this case Storey's revision of his original text at the time of production seems to have been mainly a matter of compression.) And it did prove to be the occasion of one of Lindsay Anderson's most masterly productions; seldom in the theatre can I remember being so conscious of the director's personality as well as the writer's – very much as one would expect in a film – but without the one ever being exercised at the expense of the other; the whole production was, rather, an extraordinary instance of a deep intuitive sympathy between director and writer which added immeasurably to the richness and vividness of the total theatrical experience. Characteristically, Storey, happily recognizing his debt of gratitude to Lindsay Anderson on this play and *The Contractor*, sees the great advantage of Anderson as a director in his ability to make a text work entirely in its own terms, incisively and yet leaving all lines of approach open, doing nothing to force its interpretation in any particular direction at the expense of other, equally valid possibilities.

This gift is particularly evident in Anderson's production of *The Contractor*, which came six months after *In Celebration*. Here one absolutely vital part of the play's effect – *the* vital part, one might say, since if it did not work on this level it would not work on any other – is the purely physical realization of the various manœuvres by which the tent which forms the play's centrepiece is raised. It calls for extremely detailed realism in the staging, therefore, and that is what it was given: the production benefitted to the full from the famous fascination theatre audiences find in watching something being really done on stage: frying an egg, making an apple strudel, raising a marquee. But miraculously the balance was kept between physical action and the people who are engaged in it: the preliminary fears of Storey and Anderson that critics would mostly feel: 'A very interesting tent, but where's the play?' were not at all borne out in the event.

The tent is, very palpably, a tent, but the people who put it up are, just as palpably, people, and the delicate web of relationships among them, the subtle pattern of strengths and weaknesses, understanding and illusion, which gradually emerges from the seemingly desultory banter and back-chat of the workmen as they work, has a richness and strangeness which marks it as the work of a born playwright. And this even though the raw material seems calculated to give rise to no more than a bit of harmless, superficial light comedy. Five workmen come to put up a tent for the wedding breakfast of their boss's daughter, who is marrying above her, to an upper middle-class idiot of a doctor. Ewbank is proud of his daughter's success, proud of his house and his lawn, and deeply mistrustful of his workmen, though not more so than they are of him. The setting is Yorkshire, but two of the workers, Fitzpatrick and Marshall, are Irish, a lively, exotic double act. The Yorkshiremen of the outfit, the foreman, Kay, and Bennett, both have their lives complicated by private worries, and the fifth man, Glendenning, is an amiable idiot who provides the rest with a constant, good-natured butt. In addition to his trials with his men, Ewbank has a son, Paul, who adopts the position of automatic, if ineffectual, rebellion towards anything his father does or considers important, and a tiresome old father who rumbles on about the good old days and how unpleasant today is by comparison. That is, quite deliberately, just about all the play has to it – or all it allows itself to be pinned down as having. It absolutely refuses capsulation: it is about a tent, it is about people; beyond that it can be about almost anything you like, because the image it presents, if you choose to regard it as an image, has a true poetic polyvalence – it can be interpreted in any number of ways without being diminished by interpretation or losing its validity on a basic realistic level.

About *Home* David Storey was, in advance, a little cagey: he felt he still did not know what it was about, beyond that it started from the white-table image and that a number of people came in, sat at the table, and talked. He volunteered also that we might find the play a little more technically adventurous than the previous three. That, indeed, it is. To begin with, it is, in literary terms, quite a bit slighter than either of its predecessors. *In Celebration* is a solid, substantial family drama in which the psychological premises of the action are all talked out; in the theatre the director's job was to pace it, place the nuances in such a way that we felt everything that was said was a natural, indeed an inevitable expression of this particular family's particular situation. *The Contractor* is in a way more obviously a 'director's play', in that one side of it is the elaborate physical action of raising the tent which encompasses the interior action. In *Home* virtually nothing happens externally, and very little directly meaningful is said. Its four main characters are physically very static and constantly return to the same commonplaces, the same conversational formulas in what they say. The whole play is what we infer from what they say and do, and even more, from what they don't say and don't do.

First, there is a long duologue between two respectable-looking old gentlemen sitting on the only two chairs visible in a bleak little garden. Neither has very much to say for himself – they seem to know each other, but not very well, and most of their conversation consists of generalities about the weather, clothes, people, life, and a sedulous avoidance of anything personally committing. When they leave, the chairs are at once taken by a couple of old women, emphatically not ladies, whose conversation takes a somewhat similar line, on a lower social level. If we begin to suspect that there is something a bit funny about it all, our suspicions are confirmed by the end of the first act, when the combination of the two couples in one conversation gradually reveals that they are all inmates of some sort of mental institution.

The second act, starting from this point in our knowledge, proceeds to elaborate on it slightly, but not too much. The couples are reshuffled for a while, but though the result – or apparent result: anyway, it happens – is that both men and one of the women have bouts of tears, we learn little more for certain of why they are there, where they come from, or any of the other things we would normally expect to be told in progressive revelation. The play is built of great gaping silences, and words which are hardly better, or hardly different – Pinter's second silence, when speech is speaking of a language locked beneath it. Thus *Home* is completely non-literary in its effect; it makes sense only in the theatrical situation of people on a stage, speaking and moving, and people in an audience, watching and listening, and understanding more through their instincts than through their intelligences.

This is rather a remarkable development in Storey, though his plays have been becoming progressively less literary, less dependent on the words of dialogue, for the principal effect. His strength as a dramatist up to now has been his isolation from fashion, his ability to follow his own vision unswervingly in the theatre and find to his hand precisely the right means of doing so. One could label his earlier three plays produced 'conservative' in technique if one wanted to, but the question does not arise because one never feels that there was any real choice of technique: the idea determined its form of expression, and that was that. In *Home* this remains so, even if the ideas have changed and the form of expression has changed with them. The slight flurry of discussion when the play opened about whether Storey had undergone an influence from Pinter seemed, more than usual, grotesquely irrelevant.

The play does pose a problem, though, one which the earlier plays posed in a less acute form. Of all our dramatists Storey seems to write the plays which most imperatively require perfect casts and immaculate productions for their full realization. It is difficult to imagine *In Celebration* or *The Contractor* in less distinguished hands than those of Lindsay Anderson and their original casts, so delicately balanced and difficult to bring off are their effects. But something no doubt would come over. What, though, about *Home*? What would be left, now that virtually all obvious literary content has been refined away, without a cast of the calibre of Ralph Richardson, John Gielgud, Mona Washbourne and Dandy Nichols, and above all without Lindsay Anderson to direct them? Though the individual instruments played superbly, it was their choice and blending, their immaculate ensemble, that really made everything work. It was almost like a musical performance, in which one could sense the mental presence of the conductor even though he was not physically there, directing before one's eyes. The actors seemed to be moving, speaking, falling silent, as though to some musical pattern which they could hear and we could not – and the effect was sometimes quite breathtaking. So perfect was the spell cast, indeed, that on the second night during one of the deeper silences, a mouse strolled on the stage, looked calmly around, and having satisfied its curiosity wandered off again.

Clearly, he was as much under the evening's spell as everyone else there. But that is setting a standard hard to equal. Still, whatever style Storey writes his forthcoming plays in, it seems on the cards that he will be able to command casts and directors to his measure. And whatever happens, it is certainly true that there is no dramatist in England at the moment towards whose future work one looks with more complete confidence of satisfactions in store.

Three Farceurs

ALAN AYCKBOURN · DAVID CREGAN
SIMON GRAY

We tend to expect plays by new writers to be in some sense *avant-garde*, and the newer the writer the more *avant-garde* the play. We even sometimes seem to suggest that it is the young writer's duty to be *avant-garde*, and chastise him if he is falling short of this ideal by writing straightforward, old-fashioned sorts of play. But of course, there is no necessary connection between youth and deliberate modernity. Indeed, one of the salient characteristics of the newer British drama has been exploration of a different sort: the re-examination and revivification of forms of the past, reclaiming for serious attention techniques and genres which have fallen into disuse or at least into intellectual disrepute.

One obvious example of this process is the new interest shown by several of our younger dramatists in the most 'theatrical' of theatrical genres, melodrama and farce. Sometimes, perhaps, they have been prompted to look again by the influence of Brecht, with his theoretical advocacy of the endistancing techniques natural to farce in order to induce a more critical attitude in audiences towards what is going on on stage. Sometimes, rather, it may be the influence of Theatre of the Absurd, Ionesco in particular, with its emphasis on the mechanical nature of farce, farce's shameless manipulation of its human puppets for the purposes of plotting, as a useful way of demonstrating the absurdity of the human condition. And sometimes, no doubt, it is just because the dramatists concerned enjoy traditional farce on its own familiar terms, and see no reason why they should not constructively exercise their enjoyment and pass it on to audiences supped full of horrors.

Alan Ayckbourn must surely belong wholeheartedly to this last group. Of all our younger dramatists he is the one who has most consistently and uncompromisingly avoided any suggestion of deeper meaning in his plays. Try as we may we cannot find any trace of social or political indoctrination masquerading as harmless diversion, let alone of cosmic anguish. His prime determination is unmistakably to make us laugh and keep us laughing, and all his considerable technical gifts are marshalled to that end alone. It is a tight-rope, and a particularly dangerous, vertiginous tight-rope at that, since if the writer stumbles he has no safety net of deeper significance to fall into: if his plays are not funny they are nothing. And while we are inclined to accept serious intent, however muffed, as a mitigating circumstance for a dramatist, unreasonably enough we see no merit at all in the dramatist who tries to make us laugh and fails.

Fortunately, this has not yet happened to Alan Ayckbourn. Even his less successful plays have always had at least that going for them. No doubt a lot of his basic theatrical instinct comes from the years he spent in the rough-and-tumble of provincial theatre, as actor, ASM, writer and general odd-job man. He was born in London in 1939, was educated at Haileybury till the age of seventeen, and has worked in the theatre, one way or another, ever since. Acting jobs came and went in rep at Worthing, Leatherhead and Oxford, and finally with Stephen Joseph's Studio Theatre in Scarborough, Stoke-on-Trent and elsewhere. During his time with the Studio Theatre he acted a wide variety of roles (I remember seeing him once, devastatingly, in drag as the dictatorial Cook in David Campton's *Little Brother, Little Sister*) and began to write under the pen name of Roland Allen. His earliest plays were actuated primarily by the desire to give himself show parts as an actor, but as time went on he became more interested in writing *per se*, and less interested in acting.

The first real success of his writing in this phase was *Standing Room Only* (1961), in which the elements of his later style are clearly visible. The situation undeniably has overtones of Theatre of the Absurd. The play postulates a future (but probably not too far distant future) in which London has finally become immobilized by that great, ultimate traffic jam which there is no untangling. As a result of this, thousands of Londoners have resigned themselves to staying where the jam left them, camping out in cars and buses all over the West End. The action of the play takes place on a double-decker bus stuck in Shaftesbury Avenue, and it retails a few hours in the lives of five characters who have taken up permanent residence in it with considerable comic adroitness if at times some slight sense of strain at spinning out one joke quite so far. On the other hand, it already suggests Ayckbourn's particular speciality, the comedy of embarrassment, with its characters trying desperately to continue living normal, respectable, suburban lives in these very eccentric, public conditions.

Though there was talk of a West End production for *Standing Room Only*, it never actually materialized. Ayckbourn's first West End airing came instead with *Mister Whatnot*, staged by the Studio Theatre at Stoke-on-Trent in 1963 and at the Arts the following year. The oddity of this play was that it is about three-quarters mimed: the hero, a piano-tuner let loose in a stately home, never says a word throughout, and much of the rest of the action is conducted wordlessly. The piano-tuner falls in love with a Lord's daughter, and after various vicissitudes succeeds in marrying her in the teeth of the family's objections and in spite of her fiancé, an effete but eminently suitable candidate for her hand. One might suppose that the main inspiration for the play was silent film comedy, but in fact its closest connections seem to be with the films of the Marx Brothers, and there are sections of the action which look like conscious tributes to Harpo in particular. For instance, there is a big meal-table scene in which our hero hides beneath the tablecloth and progressively eats and drinks his way round the table, to the puzzlement and consternation of the diners, who remain unaware of his presence and cannot understand why glasses and plates which, they could have sworn, were full a moment ago are now empty.

The audiences were amused, but the play got a mixed press and did not run. Not so with Ayckbourn's next West End play, *Relatively Speaking* (1967). This at once established itself as a major popular success, and went on to be translated into a dozen or more languages and produced all over the world. It is an essay in sheer mechanical ingenuity – the spinning-out of one joke beyond any reasonable possibility – and works as much on the audience's nerves (will he or won't he be able to come up with yet one more twist?) as directly on their funny bone. It thereby achieves the curious effect of being at once forced and funny. It turns entirely on one endless mis-understanding. Greg, a rather innocent young man involved in a serious affair with a not-so-innocent girl, decides he wants to marry her, and therefore wants to meet her family. She is evasive about this, but tells him that an address he finds scribbled on a cigarette-packet is that of her parents, whom she is going to visit that Sunday. So, come Sunday our hero turns up at a house in the country to introduce himself as Virginia's fiancé. But as we know, or very rapidly guess, the occupants are not her parents at all, but her former lover (an older man) and the lover's unsuspecting wife. If this were Feydeau that would be the beginning, and endless complica-tions would follow. In any case, it would be only one thread in an intricate mesh of inter-related intrigues. But for Ayckbourn that is all there is to it.

The four people concerned are the entire cast, and the whole comedy is extracted from the possible patterns of misunderstanding which can be found in this one basic situation. It has to begin with a couple of pretty obvious falsities: when Greg arrives at 'The Willows' he is made to behave as surely no young man in the world would behave, and certainly as no one as shy and socially self-conscious as he would, by marching in, not introducing himself at all (not even 'I'm Greg – Ginny's fiancé') and remaining sublimely unconscious of the total mystification his arrival causes. Why? Obviously, because the play would stop there and then if he were permitted to say any more. The comedy then derives entirely from variations on embarrassment, with the well-bred hosts trying vainly to find out who their unexpected guest is and what the hell he wants without appearing to do so. If the degree of evasiveness Greg manages unconsciously to achieve is beyond the capacity (or incapacity) of any sane person, the responses of the older couple are beautifully observed and hysterically funny.

The first act curtain, predictably enough, is the arrival of Ginny, come to satisfy her curiosity about her ex-lover's wife. (Another improbability which is a little hard to swallow, incidentally, for how on earth would she explain her appearance there without giving the game away if the unexpected presence of Greg did not remove the necessity?) Now the lady of the house feels fairly happy: here is the missing link, in that she knows Virginia works for her husband, and can therefore imagine some reason why she and her fiancé should have turned up this bright Sunday morning. But for the husband complications are only just starting. After freeing his mind of the understandable confusion that it is his wife rather than his 'daughter' ex-mistress that the young man wants to marry, he then has to cope with the problem of keeping up the pretence that the girl is his daughter for Greg while not arousing his wife's suspicions in the process. Once committed to this ticklish situation, he warms to his task and starts embroidering things for Greg with a string of splendidly embarrassing reminiscences of his 'daughter's' childhood, when she was so fat she was almost circular and was known as 'Jumbo Ginny'. Eventually, when this situation too has been milked for as many laughs as possible, all the complications get sorted out, even if no one ends up much the wiser. At each stage in the play there is present, shadowy but haunting, the feeling that the next moment it may just come to a stop, that even Ayckbourn's considerable ingenuity may run out and he will not be able to find another trick to keep things going in despite of all reason. It doesn't, and he does; the tight-rope is successfully walked even though we are sometimes too uncomfortably conscious of the abyss which yawns beneath.

Much the same could be said of Ayckbourn's next full-length play to reach the West End, *How the Other Half Loves* (1970). Here again mechanical ingenuity is the making, and at times almost the breaking of the play. The initial situation is again quite simple: we meet two families, the Fosters (upper-middle class) and the Phillipses (on their way up), linked by the fact that the husbands both work in the same firm, and that Mrs Foster is having a secret affair with Mr Phillips. The play would be quite slight and conventional, were it not for one brilliant technical device (a little like Peter Shaffer's switching of light values in *Black Comedy*) which makes it. This consists of superimposing the two households in one set, which is alternately or as a rule simultaneously the Fosters' drawing-room and the Phillips's living-room. The walls are variegated with patches of their different decorative schemes (pseudo-damask wallpaper and distemper-contemporary), their sofa and chairs mix Harrods-grand with suburban-inventive, and when the table is laid for dinner it is half linen and crystal, half paper napkins and tumblers from the shop round the corner.

This enables simultaneous actions in the two houses to be not only crosscut but intertwined. It turns out that a hapless and socially out-of-their-depth couple, the Featherstones (he works in the clerical department) have been hit upon by both guilty parties in the little game of marital infidelity as an alibi and consequently have to take embarrassing part in two simultaneous and variously excruciating dinner-parties at the same table. This sequence is the climax and really the *raison d'être* of the play. The Featherstones, almost equally ill at ease socially with both the Fosters and the Phillipses, find matters even worse when they are unwittingly forced to provide a smokescreen for Fiona Foster and Bob Phillips during an awkward dinner-table conversation which they never quite begin to grasp the drift of. Especially since they are seen by us as undergoing these two ordeals at the same time, staggering conversationally from one end of the table to the other, with the minor upsets of one occasion being picked up immediately in the talk of the other (Featherstone knocks something over in one, his hostess in the other speeds to mop it up).

But the superimposition device is used with great ingenuity throughout, as characters walk round each other, deliver insults in each other's face, sublimely, mutually unaware, and talk in apparently unrelated snatches of dialogue which nevertheless for us pick up one another, re-echoing or briskly deflating. It is only after the dinner-parties when the double set becomes single and all the complications are disentangled, that the play drifts into anti-climax. But where it is funny it is very funny indeed, with a dash and conviction which makes all question of whether Ayckbourn can qualify (on the grounds of technical innovation) as a 'new dramatist' or must be written down (on the grounds of his subject-matter and flighty approach to it) as a crass conservative sublimely irrelevant.

Not, I think that one would ever be tempted to classify

Ayckbourn as an important dramatist. He knows his limitations and seems to work very happily within them. Though not many of his plays have turned up in London, he is quite prolific, still writing plays for the Scarborough company where he started at the rate of about one a year (latest *The Story So Far*, 1970), and writing them off if they flop. He has also written a number of shorter pieces, such as *Countdown*, a sketch in the marital diversion *Mixed Doubles* (1969) about a long-married couple continuing their own interior-monologue reveries while the husband tells a joke, and *Ernie's Incredible Illucinations* (1969), a playlet for children about a boy with an embarrassing gift for materializing his fantasies. If Ayckbourn looks certain to remain, at best, one of our most reliable light entertainers, there are, after all, many worse things to be.

David Cregan, now, is a very different matter. He too has specialized in farce, and in resuscitating the techniques of classic farce within the context of the modern theatre (specifically within the framework of the English Stage Company at the Royal Court). But there can be little doubt of where his theatrical allegiances lie: he is unmistakably an intellectual playwright (which I think no one would accuse Ayckbourn of being) and his plays have made use of popular genres for anything but popular ends. In all of them, what seems to obsess Cregan above all is the elaboration of human patterns: farce, with its built-in tendency towards pattern-making, is the ideal form to give such obsessions full play. But Cregan's patterns are not entirely abstract: in the course of his plays he has some trenchant things to say about human nature, and despite the farcical surface of his writing, his fundamental observation of his fellow-men would seem to be decidedly pessimistic.

Cregan was born in Buxton in 1931, educated at Cambridge, and has worked as a teacher for most of the time since leaving university. He appears to have made a relatively late start as a dramatist, since his first play staged did not emerge until 1965, but he had already made a small mark with a novel *Ronald Rossiter*, about the slow development of a mixed-up boy into a sex murderer, as long ago as 1959. That was considered 'promising'; Cregan's first play, *Miniatures*, was far more than merely promising. It was given a production without décor at the Royal Court, but with a glittering cast including George Devine, Lindsay Anderson, Nicol Williamson, Bryan Pringle, Graham Crowden and others, which might be taken as some measure of the English Stage Company's interest in him.

No doubt influenced to some extent by Cregan's own experience as a teacher, *Miniatures* is a kaleidoscopic picture of life in a comprehensive school. Deliberately it avoids overall structure; it is built up out of tiny individual miniatures, cellular scenes which gradually reveal an intricate, shifting pattern beneath. The staff consists of old gown-wearing diehards and aggressive or cynically offhand young products of the red brick universities, specialists in the arts, the sciences and the social and economic in-betweens. And as in a beehive, there is constant buzzing to and fro, combinations, break-ups and re-combinations in an endless pattern of alliances, campaigns, withdrawals.

The ostensible cause of the trouble is precisely the question of whether or not gowns should be worn by staff. Raymond Knall, English, and Reg Parsons, deputy headmaster and history, are for; Mike Macalpine, languages, Harry Upton, science, and Amy Selkirk, senior mistress and languages, are against. Joe Johnson, music, is mostly too vague to care much one way or the other; he has a vague relationship with Joyce Pennington, English, and feels a vague sense of squalor when one of the boys, Simpson, gets punished for something he himself feels responsible for. And of all those we see buzzing about the hive, David Cornwallis, the lounge-suit-wearing queen bee/headmaster, is the least secure, paralysed by doubts about the validity of the whole school system, of education as such, and thrown into desperate immobility by the responsibility of it all. The only sign of uncertainty in this whole dazzlingly controlled first play is the very end, where a rather arbitrary suicide attempt (by Mr Johnson, bungled as usual) is brought in to mark the conclusion. But even there the curse is taken off it by the deputy headmaster's irate response to the news: 'You see how it is Raymond, he has quite deliberately spoiled the impact of my announcement. It is hard to believe that such malicious people exist.' And in general, even in its first more hesitant form (before, that is, a thorough revision in 1969) this very funny, very serious play seemed unmistakably to mark the arrival of a major new talent.

Not all of Cregan's subsequent work has altogether fulfilled the promise of *Miniatures*. It seems possible that he is, in fact, essentially a miniaturist in technique, less at ease with the requirements of a full-length evening's entertainment. Perhaps his best play of all is a one-acter, *Transcending* (1966), originally written as a curtain raiser to the earlier-written *The Dancers*. *The Dancers* is a short, tough piece taking up the beehive idea of human relationships from *Miniatures* and presenting it within the overall image of a dance. There are five characters in all. Two couples, Martin and Miss Fairclough, Mr Brown and Miss Partlett, circle each other, engage and disengage, and settle for happy-ever-after (or is it?) marriage. A fifth, Brimley, who in a sense regulates the action, is, the author says, the only one who really knows what he is doing, and demonstrates the fact by sleeping off-stage for most of the play, then returning to pick up Miss Fairclough, who is 'good at marriage', after the disgruntled Martin has divorced her. The action is a constant, ever-shifting struggle for power, with everyone changing position wildly each moment, while the element of the dance, and the varied music (accompanied by varied stage lighting which it evokes), introduces another mechanistic facet to the characterization – the people on the stage seem to vary in mood and attitude largely (like Pavlov's dogs) according to the application of quite external and psychologically irrelevant stimuli.

Transcending gives Cregan an even better ground for the demonstration of his special talents. It retails the complete plot of what might be a five-act romantic tragedy or an intricate Feydeau farce (the materials, after all, are not necessarily different, only the attitude towards them) in comic-strip form. The teenage heroine, having failed her A-levels yet again, has to cope with (*a*) parents all too concerned for her peace of mind – provided it does not take too much of their time and energy to secure – (*b*) a thirtyish bachelor neighbour with no lustful designs on her at all until it is too late, and (*c*) an elderly widower and self-styled medium who is after her and nearly gets her mother instead. All this is conveyed in marvellously confident and effective theatrical shorthand, with many asides to the audience, and flashes past to a surprising but wholly logical conclusion in which the heroine suddenly reappears dressed as a nun, in the process of taking the veil. Cregan calls it 'an obvious joke' and denies that it has any deeper significance. He ought to know, but the play remains in the memory with a disturbing undertone of something one cannot quite define. It may be a joke, but the funniest jokes are often the most serious.

This tantalizing, disturbing quality is even more evident in Cregan's next full-length play, *Three Men for Colverton* (1966). Again it is a struggle play, and again a lot of it is riotously funny. It concerns a struggle for the control, spiritual and mental, of a country village which for years has been completely dominated by a fearsome matriarch-figure, Mrs Cannock, who is now dying. In his note to the published text Cregan explains:

'The story is that Mrs Cannock wishes to preserve Colverton for ever just as it is now, and she bequeaths the means to effect this to Brother Edward. He sees Mrs Cannock's purpose as identical with his own, that is, to bring Paradise on Earth. He fails to achieve this hubristic action, but involves his two followers and the whole town in his attempt.'

That makes it sound simple and straightforward, which of course it isn't at all. Between the two poles of Colverton society represented by Mrs Cannock and Mr Dale, iron-monger and local reprobate, who stands for an anarchic spirit opposed by nature to the autocratic rule Mrs Cannock stands for, there are many factions, all eager to control the spiritual destiny of Colverton for one reason or another. The mild, ineffectual vicar, Swan, is never a very serious con-tender for the succession, though at one point Mrs Cannock toys with the idea of marrying him off to the local school-teacher, Miss Fisher, and letting them rule together. Hardly more serious is her first choice, Milend, a disgruntled antique dealer who was once an ironmonger and resents that people never let him forget it. But Father Pym, an evangelist Anglican monk (Missions to England, 1966) does manage to whip up a semblance of support in the village, and the three wandering evangelists, Edward, Dorman and Chad, do seem to have a real chance, despite occasional lapses from the straight and narrow (in Chad's case into the arms of Mr Dale, whose desires are not limited to the local nymphet Hesther), until Brother Edward unwisely dares where Christ would not to blackmail God by requiring of him a miraculous sign, and urges Chad into jumping from the clocktower in order to be supernaturally saved. The inevitable happens ('Things are more complicated than I've been led to expect,' observes Edward irritably), and the village is left without leadership, perhaps to go the way of Dale, though even he decides in the end to marry the pregnant Hesther and decline somewhat into respectability.

The manner of the play is comic, and often the way it is

written is such as to provoke us uneasily to laughter even at the most painful moments. Cregan says 'the play is not basically a comedy and must not be played up for laughs', but he accepts that it will almost constantly get laughs, and that some of the scenes which are furthest from being a joke are still worked out on the level of 'rip-roaring farce'. However one chooses to take it – and it is a play with many levels and teasing, fascinating ambiguities – it certainly requires very fast production to whisk us lightly over and through the mass of complications so that we may keep the overall image of the struggle in mind. Perhaps it is ultimately just that little bit too complicated; certainly at the Royal Court it never quite fused into one consistent image, its canvas always seeming overcrowded. But it is one of the plays of recent years which most imperatively seems to call for another production, for another more acclimatized audience, before we can come to any firm judgement on it.

Cregan's next play, *The Houses by the Green* (1968), goes off in rather a different direction, though from appreciably the same starting-place. This time the intention seems to be neo-Restoration artificial comedy, and all that side of *Transcending*'s technique – the copious asides to the audience in particular – is cunningly extended. It all turns on sex and money (the vital constituents of any holding story) in about equal proportions. Rich Mervyn Molyneux is going to give his adopted daughter Susan a fortune on her marriage. This fact has something (though not everything) to do with the interest shown in her by the neighbouring Commander – who disguises himself as a swinging denizen of the discothèques to woo her – and the butler Oliver. It also interests Molyneux himself, who is nurturing plans to marry the girl too and keep hold of his own money, assuming for the purpose the guise of a conservative landed gentleman. The plot is complicated by the suspicions of everybody that everybody else is planning horrid developments on the site of their rustic haven, the

Green, and before things have worked themselves out Susan and Oliver have also assumed disguises, and Susan has been transformed in the middle by a sudden, unpredictable bacchic frenzy at the idea of limitless procreation (unfortunately disappointed by the unreadiness of any of her supposedly passionate suitors actually to impregnate her).

The whole plot is worked out with fiendish care and ingenuity, shamelessly using obvious theatrical devices like the aside – the characters explain their motives and intentions directly to us, even though these remain consistently obscure to those about them – and the most transparent disguises, which yet effectively take in everybody else present, if not us. It is all very sharp and dry, more like an academic demonstration than an organic piece of drama, with its obsessive pattern-making, its relentless succession of reversals, transformations and mirror-images. So, of course, was *Transcending*, but at this greater length one really needs a little more flesh on the skeleton. All the same, the play is likeable, and wholly personal. Cregan, even at his least successful, has a style and a tone of voice which are all his own.

After this production Cregan was commissioned to write a brief play for children, *Arthur* (1969), which pictures 21-year-old Arthur Parson's advance to maturity from crockery-smashing, through burning down his aunt's house (on her own advice) to the vanquishing of the Fire Brigade, the female police and the local mayor (not to mention the scouts, though actually Aunt Alice disposes of them). At the end he is mayor himself, and already well on the way to being a great man. The only trouble is he doesn't fancy his former girl-friend and a devoted policewoman renounces him as too far above her, so the problem of Going out with Girls still remains unsolved. Though none of Cregan's plays has yet achieved any real success in the London theatre, he continues to write, most recently with *A Comedy of the Changing Years* at the Royal Court's Theatre Upstairs, and *Tipper*, staged by students at Oxford. He is an individual voice, and will surely be heard.

Simon Gray (born 1936) the third of our farceurs, seems to be considerably less accomplished as a sheer entertainer than Ayckbourn, and far less interesting in his ideas and techniques than Cregan. Before the first play of his to cause any stir, *Sleeping Dog* (1967), he had already published two well-thought-of satirical novels, *Colmain* and *Little Portia*. *Sleeping Dog* is a television play based on an idea which has something in common with that of Robert Shaw's novel *The Hiding Place* and his television play *The Pets*: a retired colonial administrator lures a black barman into his home in England and traps him in the cellar, where he keeps him locked up like an animal, thereby recreating in microcosm the old colonial situation he used to dominate during his career in Africa. The metaphor is vivid, but hardly stands up to examination; the play, however, got by on account of its slightly Ortonish brand of outrageousness and black humour.

The same style is developed in Gray's stage play *Wise Child* (1967), which achieved a West End production with Alec Guinness in the leading role. In it he played what seems for some time to be a rather blowsey middle-aged woman, too fond of the bottle, living with her son in a hotel kept by a homosexual. But eventually it turns out that 'Mrs Artmaster' is a man, a criminal on the run from the police; he nearly precipitates trouble by making a pass at the black maid, but his 'son' contrives to smooth it over. Eventually the tensions between them grow too great, and Artmaster, alias Jock Masters the Peabody Postman's assailant, tries to hand on Gerry to the landlord, Booker, and takes off on his own, the police still a few steps behind. Again, the impression is very much of imitation Orton, or at least Gray writes very much in the school of Orton, though the play's situation is piquant and its elaboration quite adroit – almost adroit enough to hide its essential slimness and lack of real progression.

Pig in a Poke (1969) was another television play with affinities of subject-matter, this time with one of David Rudkin's television plays, *House of Character*, which deals with the trials of a new tenant, only to reveal in the end that they are all subjective, because he is in fact a lunatic trying to make sense of the asylum in which he finds himself. *Pig in a Poke* began similarly, but this time the troubles of the couple who take the flat stem from the uncontrollable presence of a sitting tenant in the basement, who little by little takes over their home and their lives, turns out their friends, and becomes the wife's lover after beating her up (in these latter stages the affinity seems to be with Harold Pinter's television play *The Basement*, or with Orton's *The Ruffian on the Stair*).

Gray's stage play *Dutch Uncle*, produced by the Royal Shakespeare Company in 1969, continued to explore the same sort of sub-Orton territory, with an overlay of Donald McGill seaside-postcard vulgarity carefuly cultivated. God-boy, the play's timid and ineffectual chiropodist hero, has one clear *idée fixe* throughout, that he is going to match the exploits of the Dublin wife- and female lodger-murderer, and thus finally not only rid himself of his terrible missus, but also bring himself to the attention of his idol, Inspector Hawkins, and make his mark on the world by paying the supreme penalty. In putting his plans into practice he is absurdly inefficient, and though by the end of the first act he believes that he has his wife shut in a gas-filled wardrobe we know that she has, in fact, walked out and left him without his even noticing. The second act is taken up with elaborating on the situation, and complicating it slightly with the possibility that the half-witted lodger from upstairs (husband of the intended second victim) may be a local rapist the police are trying to trap through the wiles of a constable in drag. The piece seems, despite the expectations raised by the relatively exalted circumstances of its production, to be meant as a simple farce and nothing more. But as such, despite a few bright moments, it can be accounted only a fairly feeble example of the genre.

After its production Gray appeared in a very different role as adaptor of Dostoevsky's *The Idiot* for the National Theatre (1970). The adaptation was well-meant but fragmentary and inclined to skirt (perhaps understandably) the central point of the novel, Dostoevsky's discussion and demonstration of the creeping insanity of society in relation to the tormented individual. Still, the subject could hardly be further from Ortonish farce, so there is hope yet that Simon Gray may find a way of putting his undoubted skills to better, or at least more individual, use. This hope was hardly realized, though, in his next original play, *Spoiled* (1971), which sets up a triangle situation of repressed schoolmaster, pregnant wife and eager young pupil brought into the house for a week-end of intensive cramming. The petty irritations and frustrations of the household situation are quite well captured, but our theatrical sophistication proves to have rather over-taken Gray in this instance, and his final, long and slowly built-up-to shock effect, with the schoolmaster bedding the boy and being caught in a dramatic confrontation with his wife outside the bedroom door, falls with a dull thud of 'is that all?' True, there seems to be some deliberate avoiding of possible Ortonish overtones in the subject (which could be developed, for example, as an *Entertaining Mr Sloane* situation) and the character-building is sober and solid to the point of being rather boring. However, with a stronger and more original subject Gray might very easily surprise us perhaps in *Butley*, a new play in rehearsal under the direction of Harold Pinter at the time of writing.

Three Social Realists

JOHN HOPKINS · ALAN PLATER
CECIL P. TAYLOR

At one time, in the ancient history of the New Drama, it looked as though television might well be the great new outlet for great new playwrights. At any rate, consuming as much dramatic material as it did, it was a great market, and very few of the newcomers did not have at least one go at it. But few persevered. Those who got their first real break in it seemed determined to break out as quickly as they could, into the theatre, where the prestige was, and/or the cinema, where the money was. Once established elsewhere, they might occasionally be tempted back, but it would have to be a rather special occasion, suitably prefaced and presented; Harold Pinter, for instance, could hardly have had more care and attention lavished (though not to very happy effect, it must be admitted) on his last two television pieces if they had been new tables of the law brought down hot-foot by Moses from the mountain. But in general, once a dramatist had been in television, he was likely, for whatever reason, to avoid a return engagement, and only David Rudkin that I can think of has taken the unprecedented step of starting on the stage and then transferring his almost entire activities as a writer to television afterwards.

The newer wave of dramatists tend to be less rigid in their ideas, or less particular, or less snobbish – whichever way you care to put it. It may well just be that they have grown up as writers in the television era, and as far as they are concerned television is just as natural a place for a play as the stage, just as desirable a platform – especially when the stage play may never be intended for and certainly never receive the prestigious attention of a West End presentation, but simply appear and vanish again without trace at a lunch-time eat-in, as a sideshow in a political demonstration or in the repertoire of some peripatetic acting group as difficult to pin down as an old-time medicine show. If the state of the theatrical activity is healthy, the special mystique of the theatre is these days at a pretty low ebb. Hence, no doubt, the continued devotion of such writers as David Mercer, John Hopkins and Alan Plater to television, even during and after more or less successful flirtations with the stage. Mercer is, or has become, the poet of the medium, abandoning realism and reinstating the word as an equal, sometimes the dominant, partner of the image. Despite the highly personal and effective work he has done on stage, it is still possible to look to his television writing for his finest, densest, most totally achieved work. Hopkins and Plater are more prosaic.

The vital fact in John Hopkins's life as a writer is, in his own estimation and everyone else's, the two and a half years he spent as part of the regular writing team on the BBC's police series *Z Cars*. When he started in 1962 he was 31; he was born in London, had read English at Cambridge, and worked for several years on the technical side of television as a studio manager. He began writing fairly late, and in a fairly desultory fashion, had a number of short plays produced by Granada and in 1961 a more ambitious piece, *A Woman Comes Home*, done by the BBC. This observed an emotional crisis in a married woman's life (she has become pregnant by a lover, also married, has broken with him without explanation, and now has somehow to confess all to her husband) with stern objectivity, but betrayed Hopkins's lack of practice by the awkwardness with which it attempted to let us understand from people's behaviour with one another far more than it ever allowed them to say.

Curiously, on *Z Cars* Hopkins's greatest asset turned out to be his gift for making the inarticulate just articulate enough to get over everything necessary to the story without compromising the reality of the situation. Of course the series had a formula – all series have – but it was an elastic formula which allowed an unusual variety and freshness of characterization and event within the general framework. Hopkins wrote in all fifty-seven episodes, and says that meeting this considerable purely professional challenge taught him his job. In particular, it taught how to construct stories and tell them, in immediately effective dramatic terms; even the weakest of his later plays have at least had so much going for them.

Once off the *Z Cars* treadmill in 1964, he had time to write other, free-standing television plays. Some of them, like *The Pretty English Girls* (1964), were brightly negligible; others, like *I Took My Little World Away* (1965) strained too hard after significance (a cast of potential suicides had their situation rather glibly related to that of gas-chamber victims and were apparently meant to represent suffering, neurotic humanity). There was also a tendency at this time to let the choppy shorthand style of dialogue which had given *Z Cars* immediacy and pace become an uncontrollable mannerism. But other works, quieter and more controlled, showed that Hopkins was still maturing. *Fable* (1965), a controversial allegory taking place in an England where a black minority has taken over and tyrannizes the whites just as the whites tyrranize the blacks now in some parts of Africa, received a lot of serious attention and was widely enough misunderstood (despite, or perhaps because of, too many too careful disclaimers by the BBC) to start quite a storm in a teacup. More indicative, though, of Hopkins's real strengths was a roughly contemporary television play *Horror of Darkness* (1965), a sort of rehearsal for his later stage play *Find Your Way Home*, in which the apparent subject is homosexuality (a man and a woman compete for the affections of a man who is incapable of really caring for either of them) and the real subject the varieties of love and the ways love can be betrayed.

In 1966 Hopkins consolidated his position as one of the most important dramatists then working in television with his ambitious tetralogy *Talking to a Stranger*, dubbed optimistically but influentially by *The Observer*, in an oft-quoted phrase, 'the first authentic masterpiece written directly for television'. The basic idea of the plays is simple. They all present the same catastrophic day in the life of one family, the Stephenses, a Sunday during which father, mother, daughter Terry and son Alan are, for once in a way, together, but only to turn on and rend one another, and which climaxes in the mother's suicide. The four plays present four facets of the same action, overlapping one another, moving forwards and backwards in time. First, in *Any Time You're Ready I'll Sparkle*, we see it all from Terry's point of view. Terry who drinks too much, sleeps around (or has), drifts from job to job, refusing commitment and contact; and who, to make matters worse, is expecting a baby. Next, in *No Skill or Special Knowledge is Required*, we get the father's point of view, more simply expressed, for he is a simple, well-meaning man, rather cowed, always trying to be a buffer between the warring factions in his family, and now aware that neither of the children will come back and he has been married for thirty-six years to a woman who knows nothing of him, in a job he hates, in a world which holds nothing for him. The structure of the third section, *Gladly, My Cross-Eyed Bear*, is even simpler: it all takes place after the mother's suicide, and is principally a conversation piece for Terry, Alan and father, seen from Alan's point of view. Finally in *The Innocent Must Suffer* we go back over nearly all the ground previously covered, only now from the mother's point of view, seeing how all the quarrels and recriminations have reflected back on her obscure sense of guilt, anguish and insufficiency, until at the last she decides that suicide is the only way out for her. Her last words, as she dies, are 'hold me – somebody'.

Hopkins says that in writing the sequence of plays he wanted to use the possibilities of a linked series, denied him in *Z Cars* by the built-in limitations of the convention, to illuminate the same subject, the same characters from different angles, not to tell us more, but to show us a many-faceted reality from which we come to understand some of the complexities and ambiguities of life, not only what people do but why – or some of the possible reasons why – they do it. This *Talking to a Stranger* achieves remarkably well. In literary terms it is nothing – the dialogue seems flat and dead on the page – and no one of the plays is on its own specially remarkable. But after seeing all four one does have the sensation, akin to having read a densely packed novel, of having actually lived with these people moment by moment, until one knows them through and through.

Compared with this Hopkins's other television plays of the period were rather disappointing. *A Game – Like – Only a Game* (1966) was a bit like an expanded *Z Cars* about a widow tormented by a couple of small boys whose viciousness comes, Hopkins suggests, from unduly permissive home backgrounds. It built up its gloomy picture of the old woman's isolation and society's denial of sympathy to her quite skilfully before spoiling it by over-emphasis. *Some Place of Darkness* (1967) was a television opera libretto written for Christopher Whelan's music, and an adroit enough piece of simple melodrama about deprived youth drifting into violent crime. *Beyond the Sunrise* (1966) was much touted – inaccurately Hopkins says, since it had been on the BBC's shelf for some time – as 'the play he had always wanted to write', specially commissioned, posed a problem of conflicting ways of life, traditional and progressive, in modern Africa, quite fairly, but then made the mistake of introducing a suave homosexual relic of colonialist rule, now an 'adviser' to the new government, to blame everyone's troubles on. Hopkins's sense of guilt for European colonialism has been known since *Fable*, but this did seem to be going rather too far.

And then in 1968 came Hopkins's first stage play, *This Story of Yours*. It is in every way a very remarkable step forward. Its starting-point is an idea which might have come from *Z Cars*; the play in a sense could almost qualify as 'the story *Z Cars* wouldn't let me do'. The subject is a policeman who has got himself into trouble, and the professional jargon and general background of the action are, if less localized, still inevitably very much the same as in *Z Cars*. But it would be grossly unfair to assume that this is just a reworking of leftover telly material, or even an original play working along similar lines of quiet kitchen-sink realism. For the first thing that strikes one about *This Story of Yours* is that it is an intensely theatrical play. I don't mean that (as it should be unnecessary to explain) as denigration. On the contrary, it is a pleasing rarity to find a play which works so completely within the terms of a theatrical three-acter that one cannot for a moment imagine it transferred to any other medium. This is as much because of what it leaves out as of what it puts in. The play is constructed in three extended duologues. In the first act Detective-Sergeant Johnson tries, not very successfully, to explain to his wife what has happened (he has probably killed a child-molester as a result of beating him up in the course of interrogation) and to some extent why. He is calling for help – which evidently, after long years of unsatisfactory marriage, she is unable to give even if she wants to – but equally he is trying to shore up his own shattered psychological defences against the rest of the world, her included.

The second act is a long conversation between Johnson and the superior who has been unwillingly assigned to investigate the death. By now the signs of breakdown are even more evident: one minute insultingly truculent, the next Johnson is weeping and clinging pitifully to his interrogator's knees. He is sure there is something else he wants to say, but he never remembers it until too late. It is what he felt as he killed the man: at first revulsion and hatred, and then, once he had struck the first blow, overwhelming relief and satisfaction: he knew, and sensed that his victim knew, that this act embodied all the repressed, unavowed impulses of a lifetime's frustration.

This established, the third act takes us back, without more ado, to the very beginning, the interrogation by Johnson of the supposed child-molester, Baxter. This is a brilliantly conceived and written scene, as the two men, drawn together by an unconscious bond which only little by little emerges in the course of their fencing, play with each other, feint, invite, withdraw: it is, as the picture posters said of something else, 'almost a love story', and the action is played as almost a love scene, with an interior tension which can be resolved only by the orgasmic release of murderous violence.

The point of it all, in so far as it can be capsulated, lies in one throw-away line in the last act. When Jackson flings at Baxter the accusation of being a dirty pervert, Baxter snaps lightly back, 'It takes one to know one.' Precisely. Johnson is obsessed by the scenes of horror and violence he has witnessed – in the first act he pours out a terrible stream of nightmare images in a vain attempt to let his wife inside his mind. But is this because his underlying sensitivity is appalled at all this, or because somewhere in his nature is an unadmitted dark excitement which needs to be fed in this way? If he thinks he always gets the dirty jobs, he may be right, and this may be because, with his own impulses tending in the same direction, he has a particular feeling for the perverse crime – on the principle of set a thief . . . Also, like so many of Hopkins's characters, he is isolated, desperately in need of contact with someone. And paradoxically, so far are his natural feelings repressed by society that he can make real human contact only on this level, with this man, pervert to pervert, and the experience is so shattering that like the contacts at last made among the family in *Talking to a Stranger*, the only possible consequence can be violent death.

All this, when described, sounds very cut and dried: as soon as one starts writing about and explaining the play it assumes the air of a popularized psychiatric casebook. But in the theatre it does not come over like that: if Hopkins's basic framework is thoroughly schematic, he has nevertheless managed to imbue his characters with enough idiosyncratic life, to make them – and particularly Johnson – come alive as unpredictable individuals in whose behaviour a pattern may be glimpsed, rather than puppets who act entirely according to a prearranged pattern. The play is by no means faultless – it has repetitious patches, for instance, quite apart from the deliberate and meaningful repetitions, and the amplified screams and moans at the end, over the actual killing, weaken by over-emphasis a point already adequately made. But all the same it remains an astonishing theatrical début, marking Hopkins out at once, as for me none of his television plays has ever quite succeeded in doing, as a major talent.

The impression is confirmed by his next stage play, *Find Your Way Home* (1970). It takes up again the subject of homosexuality which is overtly present in *Horror of Darkness*, incidental to *Beyond the Sunrise*, and hinted at in *This Story of Yours*. The basic story this time is sheer novelette – and would be immediately recognizable as such if Julie were a woman instead of a man. Julie in point of fact is a male prostitute of (as it eventually transpires) alarmingly varied, extensive and, on the face of it, surely rather improbable experience. Alan, a middle-aged married man, has had an affair with him before, broken it off, but now decides he cannot go on with his marriage, walks out on his family and comes back to

Julie. Julie at the time is trying to dispose of his latest pick-up, and does so without too much trouble, but before long Alan's wife Jackie arrives, determined to use any weapon she finds to hand in order to bring her errant husband home. But this time it's no good; the relationship between Alan and Julie survives her onslaughts, and then survives an even more dangerous attack from Powell, the pick-up of the opening scene, who insists on reading Alan lurid extracts from the absent Julie's diaries. But even knowing all, Alan stays on.

The familiar plot is, admittedly, given a twist of surface novelty by concerning a homosexual rather than a heterosexual relationship, but it is not that primarily which enables the play to surmount some rather sticky dialogue and passages which in a heterosexual context would be dismissed as intolerably solemn/sentimental. Rather it is Hopkins's perception and revelation of a human truth behind the trite story, his slogging and sometimes exhausting persistence in ferreting out the underlying motives of his characters, all of whom, like the in other respects quite different triangle of *A Horror of Darkness*, are vaguely aware of a sense of isolation in their lives and struggle frantically to connect somehow, or at least achieve the illusion of connecting, if only in physical sex. Seen in this light, it may be doubted whether the ending is quite so glib and sentimental as it first appears; the liaison of Alan and Julie is a gesture of desperation, and it is difficult to imagine any future for it which will help to make sense of either of their lives. Also there is the calculated violence and nervous resilience of the talk, which is lifelike in its structure – its avoidance of danger points, its signalling moments of deep feeling by the selective use of cliché – but in detail highly and subtly wrought into a vital theatrical language. One may doubt the play's accuracy as a specialized picture of homosexual life, but as an image of life in general it has undeniable if slightly unbalanced power.

Hopkins's most recent television play, *The Dolly Scene* (1970) takes up exactly the same argument. Again it is about connecting, or rather people's desperate, undiscriminating and often unavailing attempts to connect. Its principal character, Anna, is in some ways a female equivalent of Julie: the office tart who really loves a married man but between whiles will go with practically anyone, abusing herself and letting herself be made the tool of other people's desires with a sort of despairing indifference through which shines a faint vestige of hope that something may happen, some contact may be made. Not that it will, not that it is; at the end we leave her precisely where she was at the beginning, with her (though only partly, conditionally her) Tom getting dressed to race off home and their exchanging exactly the same meaningless words that they exchanged in the opening scene. A hard, bleak little play, but not easy to forget.

Alan Plater (born 1935) has one general thing in common with John Hopkins – the importance of television in the development of his career – and one particular – the fact that he too worked for *Z Cars* in his early years as a playwright, and indeed stayed on after Hopkins had left, to write scripts for its spin-off *Softly, Softly*. Otherwise, though, they are not much alike. Hopkins in his writing is a passionately intense introvert, Plater an ebullient extrovert. He is a northerner by birth, born in Jarrow and brought up in Hull, where he still lives and where two of his plays have first appeared at the new Arts Centre Theatre. After leaving school he trained as an architect at King's College, Newcastle, but gave up working in an architect's office to become a professional writer when his radio play, *Smoke Zone*, was accepted for broadcasting in 1961. He has been as prolific as Hopkins, if not more so; certainly his career gives the impression of ceaseless activity, probably because his plays always seem to be undergoing transformation and adaptation, from television screen to stage or vice versa.

One of those which made the transition from small screen to stage was the first which brought Plater notice, *A Smashing Day*. Originally done on television in 1962, it was one of a cycle of plays fashionable at the time about northern lads on the prowl at the palais and northern lasses out to snare them into matrimony. But at least Plater did it well. His hero Lennie is a vague, wandering youth who never settles in a job and finds himself, more from indecision than anything else, drifting towards marriage with a girl he quite likes but was hardly thinking of in that sort of way – not yet. When she starts buying towels and being roguish about their destination he sees the danger signs, and at this moment Liz comes into his life. She is, if anything, more inclined to drift than he is, but while he worries about his rootlessness, she is easy-going and understanding. But he marries Anne anyway; the one evening with Liz is left as a wonderful memory, something not quite real. Maybe boldness, decisiveness would have let him break through to a better life, instead of allowing himself to be trapped into a drably humdrum life with Anne. Maybe, but Plater never let us think there could be an easy answer. His characters were rounded, contradictory human beings not developed at sufficient length for us to start wondering too critically about the whys and hows of the story. The success of the television production presumably prompted Plater to make over the script in 1966 as a full-length stage play. This did not prove to be a very good idea. The need to expand forced him to be explicit about aspects of his characters' personalities and actions which were better left open to our own interpretation – especially since the more he explained, the less interesting they got. This was particularly true of Lennie, who declined from a rather appealing drifter trapped by life into a dope who weakly fails to take his chances when they offer and really seems to deserve all he gets.

Other television plays of these years deal with a wide range of subjects, many of them a trifle bizarre, and none the worse for that. *So Long, Charlie* (1963) is about an eccentric artist and unsuccessful art teacher whose principal outlet is building 'shrines' in his room, to the consternation of his conventional room-mate, and tangling with the law. *See The Pretty Lights* (1963) is a simple and rather touching duologue, rather reminiscent of Marguerite Duras's *Le Square*, for two social drop-outs, a middle-aged man and a teenage girl, on a seat on a pier; it was staged in 1970, by one of those lunch-time theatre groups which, among other things, provide a happy home-from-home for short and modest television plays. *Ted's Cathedral* (1964) also later produced on stage, at Stoke-on-Trent, is an odd visionary piece about an idiot youth, who has a dream image of a memorial a self-styled widow plans to put up to her man on a piece of waste ground as a cathedral, and describes it so vividly that all about him lose their cynicism and become infected by the desire actually to build it, though Ted knows that his conception would be ruined by the corrupt world if put into execution. *The Incident* (1965) elaborated a rather pointless allegory about an England arbitrarily split in two, north and south, and a couple of brothers, one mentally deficient, who are caught, interrogated and in one case shot when they accidentally run up against one of the road blocks at the border. *The Nutter* (1965) was a jolly little fantasy about an eccentric old anarchist called Mulligan who persuades the solemn dignitaries of a grim northern industrial town to paint it white in celebration of its 150th anniversary.

With the appearance of the stage version of *A Smashing Day*, first in Liverpool then (briefly) in the West End in 1966, Plater's interest seemed to shift slightly away from television. His principal television work since then has been a trilogy, *To See How Far It Is*, about the ultimately intertwined lives of two very dissimilar characters, Murphy, a drifter who tries to make a point for his life by engaging in a flurry of pointless activities and propagating his 'law', that one's troubles are one's own, and Donkin, a public relations man who assumes the character of a Casanova but always takes flight if any of the women he so flirtatiously approaches shows signs of serious response. Plater's next stage play after *A Smashing Day* was also a reworking of television material, *Charlie Came To Our Town* (1966), which developed *The Nutter* into an amiable, rambling, quite harmless musical to open a festival at Harrogate, of all places.

The show did, however, have the advantage of bringing Plater together with the composer Alex Glasgow, and thus opening the way for his most successful show to date, the musical documentary about coal-mining, *Close the Coalhouse Door* (1968). This uses a golden-wedding party as a framework for a pattern of reminiscent song and story telling the history of the industry during the last fifty years. The people at the party step in and out of a variety of characters within the overall framework, to tell stories of death and disaster in the pits, to burlesque the ways of politicians, to engage in broad domestic comedy or to deliver impassioned oratory on strikes and basic human rights. And all through it runs the strangely contradictory attitude of the miners, which persists to this day: while professing to hate so much about the mines and their work, they are almost impossible to talk into moving away, taking some other job. The show was simple yet eloquent, and had a triumphant reception in the North, a warm enough welcome in London, and a further triumph on television.

It marks, to date, Plater's talents and his disabilities held in the happiest balance. In his attitudes he is a primitive, in much the way that Peter Terson is a primitive, but without Terson's gift for absolutely the right word in the right place or his subtle, even if instinctive, appreciation of the complexities of human nature. His follow-up musical documentary, *Don't Build a Bridge, Drain the River* (1970), also written with

Alex Glasgow, failed to make more than an intermittently lively tangle out of nearly 800 years of Hull history – perhaps partly because the show was considerably chopped about and improvised on in production. The fourth show of this kind, *Simon Says . . .* (1970), another collaboration with Alex Glasgow, fell into rather a different trap: Plater foresook documentary, however fantasticated, for the more dangerous field of satire.

As many of our newer dramatists, from John Osborne on, have found to their cost, satire is a form which requires some vigorous brainwork and the ability to see your subject straight first before you start distorting it to serve your satiric purpose. Plater's approach to the problem is embarrassingly naïve: he chooses the MCC, which could be anything or nothing, to represent the object of his complaint. It stands, presumably, for the Establishment, authority or something of the sort. Anything and everything of the sort, in fact, so that while the attack may be well-intentioned it can hardly hope to hit any particular target fairly and squarely. No more it does. Its hero is an ineffectual white-faced clown-figure, a pathetic little man called Simple Simon. In the end he seems to be winning, as Lord Thing, president of the MCC selectors (representing, Plater tells us, all that is most effete in the dictatorial Establishment), is mown down by machine-gun fire and he reads out a litany of Prime Ministers' names over the racket. But in the next scene Lord Thing is resuscitated, and Simon's boldest gesture is to contract out of a prize-giving presided over by a fatuous television commentator. It may all be an allegory of bloody Socialist revolution, a violent call to arms, in Plater's mind, but it is too diffused and harmless to strike anyone else that way.

Nor can any very sensational effect be claimed for Plater's latest work, like *Simon Says . . .* written for Hull Arts Centre Theatre, a tiny 150-seater. In *And a Little Love Besides* (1970) his target is established religion – nearly always too easy a target – and his hero is a pillar of the Church who goes slightly astray to find that everyone and everything conspires to reject him, desperately eager to keep their own hands clean. It is a comedy, perfectly agreeable but entirely innocuous because the targets Plater is aiming at don't exist, or have long since ceased to be of any real importance. In *Close the Coalhouse Door* at least he found the perfect vehicle for his talents; but in some of his earlier television plays there was the anarchic spirit of a genuine eccentric which has somehow got rather lost along the way. If he can regain either the form of the one or the spirit of the others he could do something really exciting. Betwixt and between, for the moment he seems rather lost.

Though Cecil P. Taylor (born 1929) has reversed the pattern of Hopkins's and Plater's careers by starting on the stage and taking up television, extensively though not exclusively, afterwards, in other respects he seems to belong very much in a group with them. Partly it is his journalistic background (somewhat akin as an influence to an apprenticeship on *Z Cars*), partly the genres in which he has worked – realistic social drama, musical documentary *à la* Plater. His most immediately distinctive contribution is his personal background, which is Glasgow-Jewish. But there is also his talent, which is variable, but at its best can produce drama which, in its own quiet way, stands comparison with the best the decade has had to offer.

He is at his best, I think, in *Bread and Butter* (1966), a slow-burning but finally very gripping piece. 'Gripping' sounds a curiously old-fashioned term of praise, but it is apt, for *Bread and Butter* gets full value from an element in general rather misprized by the newer dramatists (dedicated comedians apart): plot. There is, after all, something very comforting about a plot. However uninteresting we may find the characters and situations of a play initially, if we have perforce to spend a whole evening with them, it is practically inevitable that sooner or later we shall begin to feel at least a faint stirring of interest in how things will turn out, what will become of character A or B.

This is very much what happens in the course of *Bread and Butter*. Initially, the four characters who make up the cast seem uninteresting. The two men, Morris and Alec, are too broadly, simply what they are: Morris the perennial political enthusiast, haring off now after one political panacea, now after another, and Alec, the soft, silly listener to what other people say. Their women, Sharon and Miriam, are even more colourless and the background of working-class Jewish life in Glasgow between the wars, unfamiliar in the theatre, sounds much more attractively exotic than it is. Big events in the outside world come and go, but to Morris and Alec they impinge only as subjects for conversation, the groundwork on which Morris can embroider dizzying patterns of Marxist theory. The development is deceptively slow, the play almost static up to the half-way mark, which brings us to the end of the war, with Morris's fortunes on the down-grade and Alec's slightly on the up. The author's technique may seem limited and repetitive: in virtually every scene he uses to excess the old 'new drama' ploy of conversations continued at odds, with neither participant listening to the other – signifying, of course, failure to communicate or, as Pinter has it, fear of communication. Which is all very well in small doses, but continued obsessively in scene after scene can become extremely tiresome. However, by this time the plot has established its insidious hold: it has become quite interesting, in the most naïve, old-fashioned way, to know how things will all turn out for the two households.

And the second half not only answers this query, but does so far more tellingly than the question was posed in the first half. For by the end of the war, it transpires, Miriam, Alec's wife, who always did have her calculating side, has become warped about money to an extent which makes the mild, amiable Alec begin to question seriously whether, after twenty-odd years of married life, he really likes his wife at all – and decide that, all things considered, he doesn't. Not only do these two characters grow in stature and complexity, though, but so does Morris: his jealousy of Alec's quiet happiness, his dawning realization that one after another his all-purpose political solutions have let him down, his strange, contradictory relations with his wife, his family and his religion, all gradually fit together into a completely credible portrait of a rounded, inconsistent, coherent human being. Above all, the characters exist most intensely in relation to one another – particularly with Morris and Alec: the constancy of their relationship despite trials and vicissitudes, personal dramas within their respective households and changes in the world at large, is evoked with great delicacy and true, unsentimental feeling.

Nothing else Taylor has written is quite on this level of accomplishment, but none of his plays is altogether without distinction. *Allergy* (1966) is a one-acter about a Glasgow journalist torn between his Marxist principles and his hankering after private security – Morris and Alec rolled into one, as it were. His worries express themselves visibly in a disfiguring red rash which covers him when he arrives with a new girl-friend (for whom he has supposedly thrown over wife and job, though nothing is *definitely* decided yet) in a cottage in Ross occupied by a rather less complicated friend who grinds out a minority Marxist journal on his own hand-operated duplicating machine. The play is a very funny fantasia on the process of rationalization by which Christopher determines that he is actually allergic to adultery, and that really it is somehow more socialist to go back to his suburban life, away from germs and crude nature. The whole thing works beautifully in its own terms, and carries its meaning lightly, without demanding thoroughgoing 'interpretation'.

This is hardly true of *Happy Days are Here Again* (1965), which was interpreted by some as political allegory, by others as Theatre of the Absurd. Maybe it was neither, though fantasy it certainly was: the Jewish uncle of a prostitute now busy having an abortion gathers together five of her clients (a representatively various bunch including a poet, a capitalist, a cleric, a biology student and an electrical engineer) and leads them into a sort of inquest on the life of the absent tart. Symbolically (or absurdly, as the case may be) the engineer accepts the major share of the guilt, and lets the rest hang him; but then they have to deal with the moral consequences of their action. The effect was muddled and uncertain in tone; though originally written for the stage, the play worked much better in a shortened, rewritten form for radio. *Fable* (1965) is a one-act parable about a newly converted lion and a jackal discussing the morality of killing an antelope, which ends with the lion, doing what comes naturally to lions, being killed for his pains by a hunter, thereby paying for the sins of his ancestors as his descendants may pay for his. QED, but much too trite and obvious to work as drama.

An early play by Taylor, *Aa Went the Blaydon Races*, a lively costume piece about a Tyneside pitmen's strike of a century ago, fulfilled excellently its declared function of providing a piece of local pop theatre for the opening of the Flora Robson Theatre in Newcastle in 1962. A later venture into pop theatre, the musical *Who's Pinkus, Where's Chelm?* (1967) worked less well; a whimsical piece of Jewish folklore with songs by Monty Norman, it takes place in a mythical village of fools from which Pinkus, the most foolish of them all, sets out to make his fortune in the next town, but loses his way and arrives back prepared for success with the single formula that it is not enough in life just to follow the dictates of your heart. All this plot (such as it is) is disposed of in the first act, and the second is occupied entirely with elaboration and repetition. The show sadly lacked wit, point, or even a good tune or two to give it an occasional lift.

Most of Taylor's recent work has been done for television; in the three years after *Who's Pinkus, Where's Chelm?* he is said to have written more than a dozen teleplays, as well as running a writers' workshop to help budding writers, in television and elsewhere. The television plays of his which achieved most notice during this time were *Thank U Very Much for the Family Circle* (1968), a realistic but scarcely riveting account of the family life of a shifty, opportunistic door-to-door salesman (based on a more complex stage play, *Thank You Very Much*, originally written for a group of 15–18-year-olds in Northumberland Experimental Youth Theatre, which related the central character's political and personal conflicts of loyalty explicitly to the background of international events in the summer of 1914), and his trilogy *Revolution* (1970), three half-hour plays linked by a common theme, in that each depicted a notable revolutionary – respectively Cromwell, Lenin and Castro – in a crucial period on the eve of his revolution. They were solid and respectable – Taylor has put together an interesting book, *Making a TV Play*, which details the whole history of the Cromwell episode – but lacked the clear individuality of Taylor's Glasgow-Jewish-Marxist pieces. It is not merely a matter of the exotic local colour, though no doubt that helps; it really does seem that Taylor's talent goes into overdrive when it draws on his fund of first-hand experience, but otherwise is all too liable to idle and hang back.

The Legacy of Realism

WILLIAM CORLETT · KEVIN LAFFAN
CHRISTOPHER HAMPTON · BARRY
ENGLAND · ANTHONY SHAFFER
ROBERT SHAW · DAVID CAUTE

Of course, age doesn't have much to do with it. Nor, for that matter, does exactly when a dramatist arrives before the public. There is no reason at all why a dramatist of twenty, just this moment seeing his first play put on at the Royal Court – or in Stoke-on-Trent, or Nottingham, or Coventry, or wherever else it might be – should be technically any more experimental than Terence Rattigan or Robert Bolt. Nor need he be any more revolutionary in his subject-matter than in his technique. He may be revolutionary in both, but it is remarkable how many of the newer British dramatists, young and not so young, have shown themselves content, for the moment at least, to push the borders back just a little, to use the traditional methods to say very much the traditional things, with just here and there a little modification, perhaps only (though why should one say 'only', as though it is a small thing?) one new idea.

William Corlett (born 1939) is the perfect case in point. By most standards you would call him an old-fashioned dramatist. All his plays are broadly realistic in style, middle-class in their background, taking place in such unfashionable settings as a suburban semi-detached, a seaside guest house or a junior-executive cocktail party. But even with his first play to be staged in London, *The Gentle Avalanche*, seen briefly at the Royal Court in 1963, the power of the single new idea is very evident. It seems to be shaping up as a school-of-Osborne trip into *Look Back in Anger* country, with a difficult, temperamental artist in the centre being nasty to his nearest and dearest – the girl who has had the sense to move out once but comes back to the trampled on again, and the weak, weedy homosexual sidekick. Charlie is Jimmy-Porterish even in his likes: the only person towards whom he shows any gentleness is Pop, an old, retired working-man who lives in the same house. But this is where the new active principle comes in, in the shape of a mild, painfully refined young woman Charlie has quite incidentally picked up that evening in a coffee-bar. She seems harmless enough, but she is hard as nails and irresistible as an avalanche when it comes to getting what she wants. And what she wants (of course) is Charlie – but Charlie smartened up, suburbanized; Charlie transformed from a struggling painter who might or might not have the seeds of greatness in him, into a smoothly successful commercial artist. The others may struggle against her, but she knows what she wants and they do not; in this world the decision-takers always win out over the don't-knows.

Subsequently Corlett has written several stage plays and television plays in much the same style, and exploring rather the same areas of human experience, generally in very quiet, muted tones. His only real West End production, *Return Ticket* (1965), starring that well-known pillar of the *avant-garde* Sybil Thorndike, had little luck, partly because of a production which seemed to lose confidence half-way and play things for easy laughs. But again the idea is interesting: the play starts apparently all set up for melodrama, with a mysterious visitor to a seaside boarding-house proving to have had an affair with the landlady's husband, and to have come to get matters clarified, but then gradually the problems are reduced to everyday dimensions, in which real people begin to feel, however sincere they may be, more than a trifle foolish playing strong drama. *Tinker's Curse* (1968), done at Nottingham, was another strange, quiet piece, about a 17-year-old boy and a 16-year-old girl who elope experimentally and live idyllically in the wild until they are interrupted by an elderly tramp, whose arrival sets in train a reassessment and begins the painful process of really growing up. Subsequently Corlett has written three full-length stage plays, *The Illusionists* (1969), *National Trust* (1970) and *Flight of a Lone Sparrow* (1970), none of them as yet seen further south than Perth.

Some of his best work, though, has been in television, where his delicacy of touch and muted realism show to particular advantage. Most of his television plays explore one tiny incident or situation. In *The Scallop Shell* (1968) it is the bombshell announcement of a young man to his family that he has decided to become a monk, a subject few other young dramatists would care to tackle seriously, or at all. In *We Never Went to Cheddar Gorge* (1968) it is the working-out of one woman's anguish over the apparently absurd, meaningless death of the man she loved, with a mysterious, perhaps supernatural intervention in the shape of photographs which turn up showing them doing together things they never had time to do – what sounds like a terribly sentimental notion is beautifully carried off by sheer force of conviction and writing of extraordinarily spare precision. And in *The Storyteller* (1969) it is the unreasonable fears and anxieties of a pregnant woman which are talked out at a dreadful cocktail party by a young gatecrasher who seems not quite to belong to this world and anyway brings the heroine a message of peace and reconciliation. Corlett never hesitates to express sentiment very openly and directly, and this in itself gives him a special place in a generation of writers so terrified of sentimentality that sentiment itself, simply expressed, has become virtually taboo.

Perhaps Corlett is the most dedicatedly realistic of the new generation, but there are several others who began with basic realism and have never left it very far behind. Further evidence that traditional stage realism is not dead, even after nearly fifteen years of the New Drama in Britain, and the successive onslaughts of Theatre of the Absurd, Brecht, Theatre of Cruelty, group improvisation and the arbitrary happening as ideals, of sorts, held up to the modern theatre, comes from two dramatists who have achieved notice even more recently, Kevin Laffan and Christopher Hampton. Kevin Laffan (born 1922) first appeared as co-author, with Peter Jones, of a pleasant if unremarkable light comedy, *Angie and Ernie*, produced at Guildford in 1966, which brought together a mixed collection of variously obsessed people in the aftermath of bookmaker Ernie's marriage to Angie, twenty years his junior. Laffan's real breakthrough came with *Zoo Zoo Widdershins Zoo* (1968), which won critical attention and a professional production that never reached the West End when it turned up as first prizewinner of the National Union of Students Drama Festival in January 1969. It was, apart from anything else, a very suitable choice for a student group to present, since it made easy, uninhibited fun out of the situation of an Anglo-American group of dropouts living all crowded together in one Midlands flat.

The play is short on overall dramatic (or any other sort) of logic, and leaves nearly all our questions about the motivation of its characters unanswered: we never know why Bill, the basically sober occupant of the flat, lets the rest in or puts up with them for a moment, since when they have finally gone he returns happily to semi-suburban respectability with his regular girl-friend Mav; we never know why Milton, the prosperous American draft-dodger, stakes the rest of them, even though he remains in most ways an outsider; or for that matter what, erotically, Milton is up to, since he arrives in pursuit of Janet and then immediately loses interest, then seems to be making a pass at Bill, which leads nowhere either. Nor does it help that a lot of the dialogue is written in a relentless vein of gutter camp, full of bright ripostes like 'You must be joking', 'Golden glittering orbs to you' and 'Not on your Nelly, Kelly'. However, as a light-hearted, free-wheeling evocation of a certain drifting, aimless, casually promiscuous and generally lotus-eating life – particularly directed, one might guess, at a middle-aged audience who like to enjoy such things in principle, at a safe fantasy-distance – it works well enough.

Laffan's next play, and first to be seen in London, *It's a Two-Foot-Six-Inches-above-the-Ground World* (1970) is in every way an improvement. It has been compared to Peter Nichols in its making comedy out of a situation which is basically not only serious but extremely painful to those involved in it. That is actually going much too far, but all the same Laffan treats the problem of a wife with three children determined not to have a fourth, and her devout Irish Catholic husband, who can't give up sex and won't countenance contraception in any shape or form, with a breezy humour which does not altogether compromise either his intelligence or his fundamentally serious intent. Both of them come in for a bit of a beating before the end of the play, however, since the basic subject is static – the irresistible force of Esther's determination to use contraceptives of some sort, the irremovable object of Mick's piety – and everything that happens around that still centre is bound ultimately to be comic decoration – especially since there seems to be no reason why Esther should not have taken her decision to use the pill secretly ten months earlier and saved Mick a long period of unwilling self-denial.

By the end, what with the interruptions of the naïve priest Father Yeo, the coarse-grained delivery man Baker (who has been sacked from his job at the son's school for being caught by one of them, Sean, using the boy's lavatory when taken short), a more practically-minded niece and her bearded

Swedish boy-friend, not to mention the children themselves, there is rather too much, rather too farcical thrashing-around for comfort. And even at its best, in the opening scenes, the play is in no sense profound, though within its limits it has the merits of truthfulness and of appreciating that the human condition is often at its funniest when also at its most agonizing. Laffan has also been quite a prolific television playwright, usually on the woman's magazine level of *Kate*, a soap-opera series starring Phyllis Calvert, in which he was the first writer. More substantial works, more closely comparable to his stage plays, are *Lucky for Some*, a comedy with a bingo background, and *The Best Pair of Legs in the Business*, a comedy with gloomy undertones about a comedian living on a caravan site. Laffan's most interesting television play, *Decision to Burn* (1971), tackles fairly and squarely the problem of a young priest who gets a girl pregnant and then has to decide between her and his vocation; some of the pseudo-hippy chat of the girl's regular boy friend was embarrassing, but the rest of the story was handled with exemplary seriousness. Another stage play, *The Superannuated Man*, which Laffan considers his best, won a Dublin Festival prize, but had not been produced at the time of writing.

Christopher Hampton is at the moment just about the youngest playwright in captivity – a situation which has both advantages and disadvantages. He was born in 1946, comes from a settled upper middle-class background, public school and Oxford (where he took a first in languages), and wrote his first play, *When Did You Last See My Mother?* when he was only eighteen, thereby rivalling the record set by Shelagh Delaney and Michael Hastings. It was first produced by OUDS in 1966, and immediately taken up by the Royal Court and then by Michael Codron for the West End. Hampton's youth when he wrote it garnered a lot of publicity and clouded judgement – and not entirely in the play's favour. In particular it probably built up expectations for the play which it did not fulfil because it never had any purpose of fulfilling them.

It is about young people, but it is not young in the sense that it is technically experimental, puts a rebellious point of view or does anything which dramatists for fifty years before Osborne would not have been ready to do (except, perhaps, deal with homosexuality quite so straightforwardly). It is appreciably post-Osborne only in the sense that there seems to be some direct influence of Osborne on Hampton: the characters in his central emotional triangle – mother, son, and the other man who wants the son but accepts the mother as a substitute – light into each other in passages of highly-charged invective worthy of the old master himself. But formally it is hardly different from *The Vortex*, with which, in fact, it has more than a few points in common, notably the incestuously close emotional relationship between mother and son, with the mother still seeing herself as an object of desire and neither quite understanding what has hit them when a third party comes into their lives (Ian, who precipitates successive crises by trying to seduce Jimmy, succeeding in seducing – or being seduced by – Jimmy's mother, and then telling her the awful truth and driving her to what looks like suicide).

Hampton's two subsequent plays, *Total Eclipse* (1968) and *The Philanthropist* (1970) continue in the same vein of only slightly modified realism. *Total Eclipse* is a period piece in the modern manner only in that it picks as its subject, as its heroes indeed one can fairly say, two famous misfits and outcasts from society, Rimbaud and Verlaine. It covers the course of their affair from the time when Rimbaud, aged sixteen, lures Verlaine away from wife and impending family to the eventual parting, violent reunion, and an epilogue in which Verlaine hears of Rimbaud's death and reflects, in his cups, that as long as he lives a spark of Rimbaud lives too, inside him. The problem of the subject, of course, is that inherent in any study of being geniuses together: how can any but a genius as transcendent as either of those he depicts hope to convince us that they are what we are told they are, make us feel genius humming away inside these two men? Well, of course that is an impossible job, and Hampton very sensibly does not attempt it. Instead he settles for an almost documentary reconstruction, closely based on verifiable fact, of the external events in the stormy life together of the two poets. The genius we can take on trust: the extraordinary human relationship between extraordinary humans Hampton recreates vividly for us, and that is the real triumph of his play. Naturally it means more to someone who knows something about Verlaine, Rimbaud and their writings, but it is not parasitic on its subject; it takes on an independent life of its own, and is at times moving in its very refusal to tackle our emotions directly. If the overall effect is a trifle too respectful finally to take fire, at the very least it shows a conscious and highly intelligent craftsman at work on a subject which admirably suits his talents.

The Philanthropist is a considerable advance on both the earlier plays: a glittering comedy of modern manners, intelligent (again – it is terrible how the word sounds like an insult), ruthless, nervy and rather melancholy. Its central character, Philip, is a man who knows himself all too clearly for what he is: a coward, too eager to please, too fearful of not pleasing to commit himself wholeheartedly to anyone or anything outside the realm of language, in which, as a professional philologist, he is a master because he can invent the rules. The play starts with a suicide (of a disgruntled dramatist after his new play has come in for some criticism) which is riotously, painfully funny, and goes on to explore an evening of romantic disaster in Philip's bachelor-don flat with everyone ending up in bed with absolutely the wrong person (Philip with Araminta, a determined nymphomaniac; his girl-friend Celia with a vulgar but pushy novelist) for the

wrong reasons. It confirms that Hampton's talent is domin-
antly (though thank goodness not exclusively) cerebral, that
at the moment it finds the disciplines of traditional realistic
stagecraft entirely suited to its purposes (perhaps even
positively beneficial as a sort of challenge, like Philip's
anagrams), and that it promises us, in Hampton, an entertainer of impeccable skill and accomplishment. The Shaw of
the Seventies? Hardly – or at any rate, not yet. But after all,
there's no harm in hoping.

Other newly emerged dramatists seem happy to stick with
the tried-and-true formulae of the established realistic theatre
as their framework, and do not always bother very much
about transcending it. Barry England (born 1935), already
author of several television plays and two plays staged at
Coventry, *End of a Conflict* (1961), a personal drama set in a
military garrison in Hong Kong, and *The Big Contract* (1963),
about management/labour disputes in a factory, produced in
Conduct Unbecoming (1969) a surprise hit. Surprising largely
because its adroit courtroom drama set in Imperial India
shortly after the Mutiny (well-bred young officer gets
himself charged by the regimental widow with indecent
assault, in order to be dishonourably discharged, and is
defended by an arriviste bourgeois among his fellow officers,
fired with the highest traditions of regimental honour) could
have been written at any time in the last fifty years or so with
hardly a word or an action different. It seemed only logical,
therefore, that when the play was bought for filming the task
of adaptation should be handed over to none other than
Terence Rattigan.

Anthony Shaffer (born 1926), Peter Shaffer's twin brother,
came up after a number of television scripts and *The Savage
Parade* (1963), a play about a secret trial in Israel of a Nazi
war criminal which got only as far as one Sunday-night
performance, with the other big commercial success of the
same season in *Sleuth* (1970), an intricate Chinese-box of a

thriller (which is also a parody thriller) full of games, fantasies, shocks and humiliations when a famous writer of detective stories invites his wife's lover home to involve him, apparently, in vaguely criminal activity requiring him to steal some of the wife/mistress's jewellery. In a theatre starved (among other things, but perhaps most of all) of plot, *Sleuth* and *Conduct Unbecoming* became at once big hits in the West End, then big hits on Broadway, and for a while seemed to be opening in yet another language every week. Which must all signify something.

More interesting, and far more independent, though still owing a general allegiance to realism as their basic means of expression in the theatre, are two dramatists belonging to no particular group, Robert Shaw (born 1927) and David Caute (born 1936). Shaw is an actor/novelist who has written three plays as it were in the margin of his other two professions. *Off the Mainland* (1956) is about a group of characters on a prison island where all interrogations inevitably lead to execution, and about the corroding effects this situation has on the commander. *The Pets* (1960) was a neat television version of his novel *The Hiding Place*, about a couple of British airmen held prisoner by a German civilian in his cellar for years; again, one of the prisoners fears for his sanity, and the relationship between prisoners and gaoler is equivocal. *The Man in the Glass Booth* (1967), also related to a novel by Shaw, is a far more substantial and haunting work. It seems to me remarkable and effective, precisely because it does not let itself become a play about the Jewish problem, Nazi guilt, the ethics of genocide, Sadism (strictly defined) as a way of life, transference of culpability, expiation by the Way of Exchange, or any of the other abstract notions which seem to be hovering in the wings. To some extent it is a play about all these things, and more. But the extent is strictly delimited by the author's determination to make it, first and foremost, a play about a person, and a very strange and mysterious person at that, in whose words and acts these ideas are fleetingly and confusedly reflected as in a distorting mirror. The play uses ideas, but there is never any doubt who is the master.

What happens is fairly simply described. Arthur Goldman, a New York Jewish businessman, reads on his birthday that the Pope has absolved the Jewish people of guilt in the crucifixion of Christ. He begins to act strangely, makes some mysterious phone calls, vanishes and when he reappears registers no surprise that 'they' have come to get him. 'They' prove to be Israeli patriots, bent on kidnapping Goldman and putting him on trial as Colonel Dorf, Jew-murderer and war criminal. In prison Goldman/Dorf plays with them, taunting them. He is, he insists, the one German who will have the courage to tell the truth in the dock; he enjoyed his labours and is not sorry. Indeed, he adds, if Hitler had chosen the Jews instead of the Germans he has no doubt they would have followed him with equal fervour. Finally, a witness comes forward to demolish Goldman's story, and make it clear that he is after all who we first thought he was; but he, reduced to silence, refuses to leave his glass booth . . .

The question everyone asks at the end of the play is why? What did Goldman think he was going to prove? Is it just, as his accuser says, that he likes bad jokes? Is his aim to accuse his own people of complicity in their fate at the hands of the Nazis? Is he hoping to provide a model of self-sacrifice in atonement, and if so, atonement by whom, for what? Where do Christ and Hitler come into it, and what is the connection between them, and between the people they chose? Interesting questions indeed, and the more so in that Shaw does not choose to answer any of them. I say 'choose' advisedly: no doubt he could if he wanted to. It would not be too difficult to make a play dramatizing clearly and straight-forwardly any one of these questions. But it is hard to think that any neat *pièce à thèse* would go on vibrating in the memory as *The Man in the Glass Booth* does long after the performance is over. Anyone (well, more or less) can present a thesis of sorts. But to create a character as complex, surprising and, in spite of everything, as convincing as Goldman – that is something else again.

Though *The Man in the Glass Booth* is clearly more of a major work than either of Shaw's other two plays, it does share with them a dramatic interest in extreme situations. Its style is, so to say, one of abstracted realism, in that the dialogue is realistic even if time and place are telescoped in a series of rapid transitions. As for the subject-matter, it shares with *Off the Mainland* and *The Pets* a preoccupation with that borderland between reality and fantasy, sanity and insanity in which the latest generation of British dramatists seem to feel most at home. *The Man in the Glass Booth* especially is a work of considerable, if enigmatic, power – enough so to make one hope Shaw will turn his attention to the theatre as a writer more frequently in future.

David Caute is another dramatist with two other occupations: novelist and don. His first play, *Songs for an Autumn Rifle* (1961), is a complex and ambitious attempt to come to terms with the moral and political issues behind the 1956 Hungarian uprising, not only as they affected the Hungarians and the Russians in Hungary, but as they affected communists and non-communists elsewhere. The structure is very intricate, switching backwards and forwards between Hungary and London, and keeping several groups of characters in play at once – the editor of a London Communist newspaper, confused by the turn of events, his dogmatic mistress-cum-editorial assistant, his son in the army who refuses on principle to serve in Cyprus, the Hungarian rebels, good and bad, the Russian invaders, humane and ruthless. The play finally turns on the editor's decision to resign, and how he will do it, with maximum publicity or bowing quietly to the will of the party (eventually he does the latter). Caute's writing here has been accused of undue intellectualization, but I cannot help wondering if that is not largely because critics know Caute is academically interested in political theory before they come to anything creative he has done; in fact, though not all the characters are equally well realized (the women in particular are not too clearly seen), the play shows real dramatic talent allied to firm intellectual control of its argument.

The Demonstration (1969) is even better, and incidentally characteristic of its generation in its preoccupation with standards of judgement and the borderland between reality and illusion. Central to its action is the continuing attempt of a university professor to contain student protest by letting it (hopefully) transmute itself into art as a dramatic metaphor on the stage of the university theatre. Motives and intentions are constantly called into question, and realities show themselves as illusions, illusions as realities, as fact and fiction change places. The dilemma of the central character, Stephen Bright (also featured in a novel by Caute, *The Occupation*, and supposed author of an essay, *The Illusion*, both of which with the play form a trilogy under the collective title of *The Confrontation*), is that, not unfamiliar in the middle generation of academics, of trying to protect his own position, his own standards of rules, and yet come to terms with, understand and, if possible, control the turbulent ideas and emotions of his rebellious students. In this struggle he is sublimely unprepared and unprotected; he has theorized, but his students do, and the results of his ideas, or something like them, in action are unnerving. In the end it is the play *Pentagon 37*, with which Bright has tried to contain student revolt, which itself defeats him, and within the context of which he is brought to a realization of his own rejection and impotence.

Among other things, the play itself is a metaphor, illuminating many of the problems the dramatist faces if he tries to use contemporary reality as the basis of art. And one thing it makes clear: in Caute's view literal-minded realism is just inadequate as an approach to the extremes and complexities of modern experience. Not all our newer dramatists agree with him: but a significant number find that, in the world we live in today, dark fantasy and savage comedy may well be the most direct, may even be the only possible ways, of telling the truth without compromise.

The Dark Fantastic

PETER BARNES · COLIN SPENCER
DAVID PINNER · DAVID SELBOURNE
DAVID HARE · ROGER MILNER
DAVID HALLIWELL · HOWARD BRENTON
HEATHCOTE WILLIAMS

The latest generation of British dramatists are nothing if not eclectic. Between a sort of neo-academicism represented by such young adherents of the realistic tradition as William Corlett and Christopher Hampton, and the determinedly non-realistic manner of, say, Howard Brenton, with his dramatic strip-cartoons, there is a whole range of styles, dictated, obviously, much more by individual taste and inclination than by any overall notion of what is and what is not fashionable in the modern theatre. In this, of course, the newest generation remains true to the pattern established by the New Drama right from the start: a 'movement' which would embrace right away John Osborne and Ann Jellicoe, Arnold Wesker and Harold Pinter, N. F. Simpson and John Arden, might have many accusations levelled against it, including that of being too various to be regarded as a movement at all, but at least it could not be accused of conformism, timidity or undue regard for the merely voguish. The same is true right up to the most recent batch of new arrivals.

All the same, some sort of pattern can be faintly discerned. These are obvious connections, for example, linking the work of Peter Barnes, Colin Spencer and David Pinner, all of whom have distinguished themselves in a kind of baroque black comedy, related in its turn to the plays of Joe Orton, though more expansive and extravagant than his, after all, rather neat, classical work. There are other links between the plays of David Halliwell and of Howard Brenton or of Heathcote Williams, with their interest in the rhetoric of insanity and the social comedy of the monstrous act. And these in their turn could be linked back to Charles Wood or Edward Bond or David Mercer. And other, more isolated figures like David Caute and Robert Shaw could also fit in here, with their dramatic interest in extreme situations, in the borderland between fact and fantasy, in their determination in their plays to give full value to the many facets of human experience, the subjectivity of human judgement.

Indeed, if one were to see one central thread in the newest of the new drama, it would I think have to be the question of judgement, of the possibility of standards of judgement. Again and again, these dramatists are attracted to such subjects as child murder, sex murder, rape, homosexuality, transvestism, religious mania, power mania, sadism, masochism. And though the angle of approach to these subjects varies enormously from play to play and writer to writer, one thing at least we may be sure about in advance: that it will not be any easily predictable, accepted angle. Of course (we can now say) there will be no direct moral disapproval – the child molester or necrophile or whatever may well indeed be the most sympathetic character around. But also, we may feel fairly confident, these – as they would once have been pigeonholed – 'social problem' subjects will rarely if ever be approached as social problems, for solemn, semi-sociological or psychological dissection. The characteristic tone is outrageous comedy, and even in the most overtly serious treatments of this kind of subject outrageous comedy keeps on somehow breaking through.

In the plays of Peter Barnes (born 1931) the comedy

predominates from the start. Or at least it does in *The Ruling Class* (1968), the first play of his to make any kind of a splash, though by his own account he had been a playwright for ten years and a screenwriter for fourteen when it appeared. It is, as a matter of fact, possible to catch up with earlier works of his among the low-budget cinema thrillers which turn up every now and then late-night on television, but I don't suppose he feels any important creative responsibility for films like *The White Trap* (a convict on the run trying to be with his wife when she has her baby). His 1960 television play *The Man with a Feather in his Hat* was a bit more recognizable in the light of his later work: a burlesque trial drama in which a man is accused of murdering his mistress and no one turns out in the end to be exactly what he seems.

But *The Ruling Class*, described as a 'baroque comedy', is a sort of glittering satirical charade holding up a distorting (or is it so distorting?) mirror to the English aristocracy. The thirteenth Earl of Gurney accidentally hangs himself in the midst of an intricate fetichistic exercise, and is succeeded by his even dottier son, a Franciscan and part-time religious maniac. Before long he becomes a full-time religious maniac, and is put away for treatment by his family. Meeting another self-appointed messiah face-to-face, his mania takes on a sadistic turn, which makes everything all right: while he believed himself to be the God of Love of course everyone thought he was mad, but now he sees himself as a vengeful Jehovah condemning sexual impurity and advocating corporal punishment he is judged to be a perfectly normal member of the aristocracy and takes his pre-ordained place in a mummified House of Lords without further ado.

Barnes's subsequent work has included a double bill performed at the Open Space in 1969, *Leonardo's Last Supper* and *Noonday Demons*, and a conflation-adaptation of Wedekind's *Erdgeist* and *Die Büchse der Pandora* into one play, *Lulu*, for Nottingham Playhouse (1970). The Wedekind must obviously have been a labour of love, and one can see, if not necessarily a source for, at least a striking likeness with Barnes's own brand of coolly ferocious comedy in Wedekind's ruthless analysis of the socio-sexual power-structure he saw around him. *Leonardo's Last Supper* is a briskly ironic fantasy which imagines Leonardo, prematurely carried off to the charnel house, waking up and being killed off again by the attendants when he refuses to pay his dues. *Noonday Demons* takes up one episode of *The Ruling Class* in a different context: a first-century anchorite suffers a series of routine temptations, then (shades of the Earl of Gurney's confrontation with a rival messiah) a mirror image of himself, whom he challenges in a succession of acts culminating in murder, all in the name of Christ.

Barnes, at least, seems to have hit with comforting certainty on the right tone for his sharpest observations. Colin Spencer (born 1933) attempting something of the same in *The Ballad of the False Barman* (1966), a wild and wayward musical fantasy about a bald lesbian running a bar-cum-brothel, a male prostitute, a transvestite, disguises and last-minute revelations of parentage, but went rather far astray, losing the (apparently intentional) overtones of Brechtian comment on society in a lot of peripheral camp fantasy. His next play, *Spitting Image* (1968), brought its material into focus much more effectively: it was a happy little piece about a couple of homosexuals who find out that they are expecting a baby.

At the opening Gary, the softer of a loving couple of five years' standing, is grotesquely swollen. Tom thinks he should do exercises to reduce, but Gary is convinced, despite all argument to the contrary, that he is pregnant. And so, as it happens, he is. He is delighted when he is operated on and delivered of a bouncing baby boy. Tom is, all things considered, less happy, and the authorities are not happy at all. To begin with, it is all so untidy, men having babies without wives; it does not fit in with the established pattern. And then, what will happen if others get wind of it? They have, after all, gone far enough, probably a lot too far, by legalizing the whole disgusting business. But what if lots of these wretched perverts now take it into their heads to reproduce? The answer, obviously, is to have the child adopted and hush it all up. But Gary is adamant. It is his baby, and he is going to keep it. The couple weather various attacks, direct and indirect, before Tom finally succumbs to the emotional blackmail of his now widowed mother and Gary agrees, in the hope of making contact with other homosexual mothers, if they exist, to go with his baby into hospital for observation. What follows involves broken promises, eleventh-hour rescue, the triumph of a band of militant homosexual mothers, and a neat little twist in the play's tail, with Tom now expecting while Gary proudly looks on. It is very jolly, very happy, an immensely pleasant and holding way of spending an evening in the theatre.

But is it any more than a light-hearted piece of camp fantasy? Surprisingly enough, it is. Colin Spencer has learnt from the acknowledged inspiration of the novels of Ronald Firbank that camp nonsense can sometimes cut deep. And in this play, without ruffling the surface too much, he has managed to do two quite difficult, serious things as well. One is to use a fantastic particular instance in order to illuminate a believable, disturbing reality. If the birth is fantastic, the opposition Gary and Tom encounter, the ways and means by which the authorities seek to suppress the awkward individual, the special case which obstinately refuses to fit into the nearest convenient pigeonhole, are all too uncomfortably credible. The fantastic particular is made to stand effectively for a host of less eye-catching realities, and the social satire reaches its target unerringly.

The other difficult thing Spencer does impressively is to create an entirely believable married couple, living and growing together and apart. Few heterosexual plays have done this so well, though essentially the reactions of the two parents here to their joy-cum-problem are no different from those of many a more normal married couple. The father's conventional pleasure at fatherhood mixed with resentment at the loss of freedom, the ties, the expense, the transfer of his partner's attention from himself to the child; the mother's at first total absorption in and joy over the child, then the gradual shaking-free, the returning consciousness of external reality. All this, for all the play's cheery light fantastic, is finely and precisely done. The play, however it may look at first glance, contains altogether more truth than is quite comfortable.

David Pinner (born 1940) seems to be attempting something of the same genre in *Fanghorn* (1967), a 'purple comedy' about the incursion of a sadistic lesbian into one of those normal suburban homes where father is symbolically making love to daughter during fencing practice while mother joins in to make it an incestuous threesome. Fanghorn herself is determined to humiliate the male by reducing him to a subservient role through tying him up, whipping him with a bullwhip, and symbolically castrating him. Critics and audiences were rather puzzled as to whether this was all meant as a self-sufficient comic extravaganza, or a burlesque on the drama of Genet, or possibly both; at least there seemed to be fair unanimity that it succeeded as neither. Otherwise Pinner has written in an alarming variety of styles, his three best-known plays, *Fanghorn*, *Dickon* (which began life as a radio play, 1966) and *Drums of Snow* (1968) resembling one another in little but a weakness for verbal extravagances, intricate flourishes of metaphor which give even the relatively straightforward plot of *Dickon* (a middle-aged man is dying of cancer, knows it, and has to try, along with his family, to live with the knowledge) a surface of baroque elaboration. The *Drums of Snow* seems from reading (I do not know of any stage production) to be a slight improvement: at least the historical background (the play depicts the life and ideas of John Lilburne, leader of the extreme republican faction in the Commonwealth during Cromwell's rule) provides a discipline of sorts, and is accepted, rather illogically no doubt, as some justification for speech more ornate than we are used to in the theatre these days. But it is hard to see from these three plays how Pinner will develop, or to predict whether he will manage to pull his varied talents together into a coherent artistic personality.

In his taste for rather overblown poetic dialogue Pinner has some slight resemblance to another young dramatist, David Selbourne (born 1937), though for Pinner's apparent yearnings towards Theatre of Cruelty Selbourne substitutes a surprising amount of sweetness, whimsy and even flagrant sentimentality. The mixture is present in the earliest play of his I know, *Samson* (1967), which depicts Samson's growth towards manood in a series of heavily poeticized encounters with sex and the grown-up world. Selbourne's best-known play, *The Play of William Cooper and Edmund Dew-Nevitt*, produced in Exeter in 1968, handles rather the same subject in rather the same style, though this time the hero is a simpleton with a peculiarly tiresome line in free-verse baby-talk and a quite inexplicable fascination for everyone else in the play. Later works include *The Two-Backed Beast* (Liverpool, 1968) a rather fancy and overblown parable about power and freedom in an imaginary domain; *Dorabella* (Edinburgh, 1969), a somewhat sentimentalized comedy-drama about a fifty-year-old spinster who tries to live out her fantasies of love with her hairdresser's boy friend and doesn't get at all what she bargained for; *The Damned* (written in 1971), a fantasy of human patterns forming and re-forming among seven characters, all exemplifying the big abstractions of Life, Love and Death; and *Alison Mary Fagan* (1971), a wordy monodrama about the outer and inner life of an actress. Though some of his preoccupations are fashionable, and his vocabulary extends to include the hip jargon of the hallucination generation, essentially, and quite anachronistically, his main ambition seems to be to take up British drama where Christopher Fry left it: 'It's the lyrical impulse which interests me. And it's only that which I think can establish the relationship with the audience. In my belief theatre is to to do with language, ideas, and communication – not with devices, mystification and ritual.'

Which is all very well in principle; almost anything is all very well in principle. But after the windy verbal extravaganzas of David Selbourne it comes as rather a relief to turn to *Slag* (1970), the first play by David Hare, who was born in 1948 and is consequently the youngest playwright dealt with in this book. Here stage directions are reduced to a minimum and the dialogue itself is pared to the bone. There are just three characters, teachers in a girls' school which appears variously as a jolly home-from-home (to Ann, the headmistress), a fertile breeding-ground for a Women's Lib revolution (by Joanne, the doctrinaire young virgin), and a man-less desert (by Elise, the mildest, most middle-of-the-road member). It also appears from time to time as a prison from which none of them can escape. At the beginning the three take a vow of celibacy in the cause of revolution, but before long they are bickering among themselves, and as things get wilder and wilder the pupils leave one by one, hints of a lesbian pregnancy develop, and finally, after deciding that there is nothing left to keep them together, the three apparently decide anyway to start all over again. It is all very strange, very funny, and quite violent in both word and action. Also, several female critics guarantee its uncanny accuracy in mirroring the way women together alone think, feel and talk. On the strength of the play David Hare has been signed on as resident dramatist at the Royal Court.

In *How's The World Treating You?* (1966) an older, and in outlook and approach quite a bit more conservative playwright, Roger Milner (born 1925), seemed to be approaching rather the same sort of dramatic territory as Barnes, Spencer and Pinner in *Fanghorn*. Its hero's fantastic progress starts in a military transit camp where he arrives in running shorts without the two hundred men he was commanding, who have somehow vanished without trace. From there on he undergoes in the next twenty years a succession of major and minor disasters, teaching, marrying a pupil and becoming a washing-machine salesman, and in the end, rather comically, kills himself. The play is loosely-knit and episodic, but with a dotty wayward charm a little like Henry Livings's *Stop It, Whoever You Are*. Previously Milner had hit something of the same form in *Upside Downing Street* (1963), a farce about an MP who has always attended the House regularly, without speaking, for the last thirteen years, and suddenly finds himself the only surviving member when the rest are wiped out in an explosion at a secret session he is unable to attend. That was never produced in London; it is a pity London has not yet either seen any successor to *How's the World Treating You?* from Milner's pen, though a new play, *Eat the Cake and Have It*, opened in Nottingham in 1970.

By comparison with the flightier fantastic comedians David Halliwell (born 1937) cuts rather a serious figure. But only in such a context, let me hasten to add: nearly all his plays work through comedy, of a, by conventional standards, fairly outrageous character but not either camp or fliply 'black'. His most famous play, *Little Malcolm and his Struggle against the Eunuchs* (1966), remains in many ways his best, perhaps because it is technically among his most uncomplicated. It seems, indeed, to tell its story in quite a direct, realistic way, and it is only from the story itself, and the tone of the recital, that we begin to suspect there is something else in Halliwell's mind.

Malcolm Scrawdyke has just been expelled from Huddersfield Tech on account of his bad influence on other students.

In the course of the play we see this at work on a group of his old pals. He starts a totalitarian party of four, in order to stage a fantastic putsch in which the principal who kicked him out will be blackmailed into destroying a painting pinched from the local art gallery, and thus exposed to public ridicule and obloquy. Two of the three disciples go along with this, and the third would, were he not, as a born victim, expelled from the party on equally fantastic grounds of conspiring with the enemy. The main achievement of the three remaining is, egged on by Malcolm, to beat up fairly effectively a girl he is drawn to but too shy to get anywhere with and who commits the additional crime of seeing through him. When the time for the planned putsch comes, though, Malcolm cannot go through with it; he is deserted by his followers and as the curtain falls is seen leaving his gloomy attic studio to phone the girl, apologize if he can, and maybe start over again. The play is gripping and effective whenever Malcolm is talking to himself, or carried away by his own eloquence when talking to others. But when the whole thing is moved from subjectivity, when Malcolm is seen in relation to other people, acting and reacting, the play at once falters and loses direction: the physical enactments of fantasy (a continuing preoccupation of Halliwell's), like the theft of the painting and kidnapping of the principal, rapidly become tiresome because they tell us nothing about the characters and lead nowhere in the plot; they are decoration applied to no sufficient base, time-fillers which only pad out a play already too long for its material.

The exact intention of the play is not immediately obvious. It may be intended as a parable about the origins of fascism, exemplifying all the right Boy Scout notions about the biggest bullies being the biggest cowards and collective violence being rooted in individual weakness. Certainly it concludes with an unexceptionable if rather square and old-fashioned moral being resolutely thumped home. But the trouble with the play as a think-piece is that it just will not bear this sort of weight. The characters are too *outré* and too improbably situated for us to be able to accept any general conclusions from their individual actions; to make this sort of generalization from the particular, after all, you have first of all to convince audiences that the particular instance is completely believable and that the books have not been cooked in any way.

Equally, the objection to the characterization comes up if the play is meant – this seems to be the main alternative – as a human interest story. The chief problem here is the central figure, Malcolm. The play gives every sign of too close an identification between author and his hero. It is not absolutely simple, in that Malcolm is not merely idolized or sentimentalized: he is flattered first in his power and magnetism (it is impossible to believe that Malcolm, as we see him, could have exerted such unchallenged influence on his contemporaries and been accepted so uncritically as a giant among men, yet we have the disinterested testimony of the girl that he was), then in his downfall, which has the sort of extravagance and exaggeration one associates with True Confessions, in which it is *infra dig.* to settle for being anything less than the worst of sinners. Still, a lot of the talk works superbly; as a pourer-out of theatrical eloquence Halliwell has had few equals since Osborne.

Since *Little Malcolm* Halliwell has been busy with helping to run the Quipu Company in various homes and various guises, writing plays and playlets for them, writing for radio, and turning out one more major work, *K. D. Dufford Hears K. D. Dufford Ask K. D. Dufford How K. D. Dufford'll Make K. D. Dufford* (1969). All his writings are very much of a piece, even the most informal, like *The Experiment* (1967), a satirical entertainment devised and directed by Halliwell and David Calderisi which used the assassination of President Garfield as a jumping-off board for a series of supposed improvisations by various members of an acting group, each setting out to dramatize the happening in a different way: as a piece of sub-Jooss ballet, then in Warner Brothers style *c*. 1938, then as theatricalist theatre scattered all over the auditorium, then as silent comedy, theatre of fact, poetic drama, psychological drama, epic theatre and finally the director's own pet notion, infra-theatre, designed to bore audiences so much that they will return to find their own drab lives outside the theatre transfigured in comparison.

Murder and varying viewpoints on the same events are two abiding Halliwell interests in drama: the varying viewpoints come up again, quite obsessively, in *K. D. Dufford*, which tells the story of Dufford's attempts to make a name for himself, largely by planning and carrying out the murder of an eight-year-old girl. He is a figure in the same paranoic mould as Malcolm, seeing himself as an unrecognized superman, and all the stages of his plan are seen through his own eyes. But we also see them as his contemptuous companion Thagney sees them, and as the eventually bereaved parents see them. It is an interesting idea, and the play yields passages of extravagant invention and wildly grotesque comedy in Halliwell's best manner. But the structure finally becomes a trap, since not everything that happens is sufficiently interesting in itself to bear at least four full accounts of it, nor are the four viewpoints always sufficiently differentiated to give us new insights each time.

Muck from Three Angles (1970) is shorter and sharper, gaining from being played out entirely in terms of comedy. The event here is the visit of a crazy salesman insisting that he is selling a caseful of rubbish for God to a housewife and her best friend; what happens – and more especially the people it happens to – is shown to us from three viewpoints, those of the salesman, the housewife and the friend. The result is mechanical but very funny. *A Discussion* (1970) is a short duologue between a husband and wife quarrelling in a bathroom – about what we never discover – and is equally shrewd and entertaining. But Halliwell is undoubtedly at his best and most individual when taking the extraordinary character, the lunatic or the murderer, and asking the linked questions with which *K. D. Dufford* opens and closes: 'How was he different? How am I the same?' In *Little Malcolm* and *K. D. Dufford*, for all their occasional longueurs and irrelevancies, there are moments of painful comedy worthy of Gogol at his best: they make you laugh, and think while you do it.

One of Halliwell's lighter pieces, *A Who's Who of Flapland* (originally a radio play in 1967), made up a double bill at the Royal Court with *Christie in Love* (1970), the play in which Howard Brenton (born 1942) comes closest to him in subject-matter. But while *K. D. Dufford* is extravagantly expansive, a hold-all of a play, *Christie in Love* is pared down to absolute essentials, into the dramatic equivalent of a strip cartoon. Brenton is, if not resentful, at least rather puzzled at the recurrent comparison of his dramatic method to that of a strip cartoon, since he disclaims any particular interest in strip cartoons or any conscious influence. All the same, the comparison is irresistible. Psychology and explanation are ruthlessly suppressed, dialogue is reduced to the skeleton indications of a cartoon's bubbles, the action of his plays proceeds from image to image with virtually no transitions, no gradations.

Christie in Love, originally presented on tour by the Portable Theatre in 1969, is a perfect case in point. The action a sort of Chinese box: on the outside is almost a literal box, a compound of chicken wire scattered with rubbish in which Christie's victims wait to be dug up by the police and in which Christie himself is finally buried. Inside this burial-ground box is another box, that of Christie's interrogation by the police. And in that is another, the flashbacks of his confession. Thus image follows image, image is sometimes superimposed on image, and when the horror becomes too direct the police (representing presumably, among other things, society at large) turn aside into blue jokes, as though to cancel out horror with protective humour. Again, as in strip cartoons, obvious visual equations can be made without inquiring too deeply into the reasonable basis of the equation: it is enough simply to present Christie as a suffering weakling, the police officer as a fascistic thug, and leave it at that.

Much the same approach to drama informs the best-known of Brenton's other plays, *Revenge* (1969), first performed at the Royal Court's Theatre Upstairs. In fact the revenge, or desire for revenge, is twofold: Adam Hepple, a lifelong criminal, conceives a passionate desire to revenge himself on MacLeish of the Yard, the policeman who has always, as he sees it, victimized him. But when he shoots a policeman MacLeish becomes equally impassioned in his vengeful pursuit of Hepple. The tone of the play veers wildly from melodrama to farce, up to a curious conclusion in which both Hepple and MacLeish die quietly in their beds, all passion spent. In performance the roles of Hepple and MacLeish are played by the same actor, doing a succession of quick changes – which all adds to the fun of the thing, if not I think to its significance.

The method is obviously limited, but in a theatre which sometimes seems in danger of sinking altogether under its load of subtlety, refinement and civilization, Brenton's avowed desire to use drama just as a way of 'stirring it up' is enlivening. In practice his method is erratically successful. Two of his short plays, *Heads* and *The Education of Skinny Spew* (1969), show it at its compressionist best. *Heads* is a bleak little comment on the relations of the sexes, in which a monstrous young woman with two possible lovers, a muscle-man and an intellectual, briskly decapitates them both and switches heads – only to find that eventually the two resultant men still gang up on her. *Skinny Spew* is the life-story of a Blakean baby who nurtures the urge to revolt in his cradle and develops instantly into a figure of monstrous savagery and determination. Both plays are frightfully funny, and manage perfectly to say what they want to say within their length, without outstaying their welcome. The same cannot be said for *Fruit* (1970) in which Brenton lays about him with too single-minded relish at the expense of all politicians, public figures and people in authority, denouncing them as corrupt from the angle of wholehearted anarchism. The central character is an embittered osteopath who has come across all their secrets in the line of professional duty; this might make a good starting-point for satire, but instead the piece is reduced to an hysterical succession of violent set-pieces, so unorganized that monotony and boredom rapidly supervene.

Brenton is clearly a hit-or-miss dramatist who hits often enough to be worth watching. Heathcote Williams (born 1941), dealing with rather the same areas of life in his two plays, *The Local Stigmatic* (1966) and *AC/DC* (1970), is on the contrary a very conscious, deliberate writer, and in his own way an extremely careful literary craftsman. 'He's like Congreve,' William Gaskill rather alarmingly volunteered during a broadcast discussion, and though the comparison seems far-fetched one can see what he means. The same obsessive regard for the exact placing of words, the same unreliability in calculating the overall dramatic effect of the words, the same tendency to let his characters' eloquence carry him beyond their words' dramatic value. The fault is less apparent in *The Local Stigmatic*, a one-act play of considerable verbal and physical violence, almost entirely unexplained. In fact the only assumption one can make, considering the play in even faintly realistic terms, is that all the characters are mad.

Probably that is right enough, if we look back from it to Williams's extraordinary book evoking the lunatic half-world of Speakers' Corner fanatics, *The Speakers* (1964) and then forward to his play *AC/DC*. In *The Speakers* Williams re-creates, with extraordinary powers of mimicry, the world – or rather the separate, self-defining, independently co-existing worlds – of a number of speakers at Speakers' Corner, all with some pretty weird bees in their respective bonnets. *AC/DC* is in some respects an extension of the technique, an exploration of some further aspects of the same theme. And here, as in the book, the miracle is how far the author has managed to write himself out of his work, to present us with a powerful picture of some very strange people with very strange ideas and leave it absolutely to speak for itself, without explaining, apologizing, hinting by the flicker of an eyelid at what sort of response we are expected to make.

The result is at once exhilarating and extremely wearing. I cannot decide with the play – as I could not with the book – how far the obstacle-course side of it is deliberate, whether it is intended to be quite so much of an ordeal as from time to time it is. Certainly taken bit by bit the play is astounding in the virtuosity of its writing, but taken as a whole it has passages of monotony and tedium which test (and are perhaps designed to test?) an audience's patience to the utmost. Particularly in the first act, the one labelled 'Alternating Current'. Maybe it is because, in writing the roles of the vaguely hippy couple in the amusement arcade, Williams has slightly overplayed his hand in order to demonstrate the emptiness of their heads and the hollowness of their life-gesture (they are, as their companion Sadie eventually observes, essentially the perennial conventional 'Mr and Mrs America', only, this being 1970, the conventions they blindly obey are rather different): audiences are likely to come to that conclusion and wish them away some time before anyone on the stage does.

The most gripping part of the first act is that which most clearly prefigures the second, 'Direct Current': the long monologue given to Maurice in which he describes in considerable detail his experiences with a couple of psychologists interested in using hypnotism to demonstrate the reality of reincarnation. This section gives the actor a great rhetorical opportunity; it is very persuasively written, with a vivid sense of theatrical timing. In the second act we come back to Maurice and his obsessions – especially as they concern his friend/lover/doctor/patient/master/slave Perowne, and in so far as they chime with the obsessions of Sadie, whom they have persuaded (involuntarily) to abandon her menage with Mr and Mrs America and butt in on their lives instead. Clearly, in a sense they are all mad, just as the Speakers are all mad: that is, they hold to ideas which are not widely subscribed to elsewhere, which, perhaps, no one but themselves believes in at all. It is all to do with the conservation and right use of energy in the universe, the waste or misuse of energy through the work and the adulation of pop stars, the vampiric effects of the mass media, drawing energy out of the individual members of the public subjected to them – that sort of thing.

And of course this does pose a problem for the dramatist: insanity in drama, as in literature in general, tends to become boring to the degree that it inhibits us from making connections between what we see or read and some thought or experience of our own: it can feel very like being in a party where everyone else is playing a game of which one knows neither the rules nor the aim. To overcome this is a matter partly of technique, partly of sheer confidence. Technically the talk has to be good enough, taut enough, written with a sharp enough dramatic sense to keep us listening in spite of ourselves; but more important, whether we understand or not, we have to be convinced by the confidence with which the participants play the game that it has rules, that they know what they are doing, and that, in their own minds at least, they really are going somewhere. This, in the second act, Heathcote Williams does superbly well. Maurice's description of how he savaged a doctor who would not give him electro-shock treatment by means of a species of psychic attack, or Sadie's progressive destruction of a collage of mind-eating figures out of the pop culture pantheon, or her trepanning of Perowne and orgasmic exorcism of Maurice's fantasies, work shatteringly well as theatre. So well that any question of what they do or do not 'mean' seems sublimely beside the point.

In any case, the play is a *tour de force*, whichever way one looks at it, and for all its frustrations and irritations a compelling piece of theatre, sometimes wildly funny, sometimes haunting. And in it, curiously, extremes meet: Williams is regarded in some respects as our most advanced dramatist, and yet in his meticulous concern for the written word, his almost painfully acute sense of style, he could also be seen as the most traditional of them all.

Epilogue

It is customary to conclude studies of this kind with some sort of rounding-off summary, pointing out lines of continuity, suggesting lines of development, packaging the subject neatly for easier consumption. But in this case it is just not possible; that, indeed, is one of the major excitements of the present theatrical situation in Britain. Though most of the latest generation of arrivals have their own distinctive styles and areas of interest, so that it is just about possible to hazard a guess about the direction in which any one of them may develop, there is little or no consistency of vision or subject-matter from one to another. 'Trends' are conspicuous by their absence, and a dramatist newly making his mark today may do so, like Howard Brenton, somewhere on the outer fringe of the professional theatre, or outside it altogether, like Kevin Laffan with *Zoo Zoo Widdershins Zoo* (first produced by a student group and noticed at a student drama festival); on the other hand he may, like Barry England with *Conduct Unbecoming*, strike lucky with a thoroughly conservative well-made play presented right in the heart of the commercial West End.

Nor is it even possible with too much certainty to line up places of arrival and the kinds of play which arrive: if the West End remains on the whole reliably conservative in its choice of plays (oddities like Peter Barnes's version of Wedekind's *Lulu* plays have to be thoroughly tried out elsewhere before anyone will give them a West End whirl), the less established outlets are not necessarily exclusively wedded to experiment – *Zoo Zoo Widdershins Zoo*, for example, is not exactly the last word in dramaturgic modernity, nor is

Tom Stoppard's *After Magritte*, despite its initial presentation at a vaguely advanced lunch-time theatre.

There are, it is true, a number of themes which seem to run through the work of a fair proportion of the dramatists who have emerged in the last five or six years. No doubt this is partly due to external circumstances, particularly the long-awaited disappearance of the Lord Chamberlain's censorship, which has at last made these themes acceptable. The – by the standards of earlier British drama – extreme violence of word and action in plays like Edward Bond's *Saved* or *Early Morning*, Charles Wood's *Dingo*, Heathcote Williams's *AC/DC* and others is partly no doubt an expression of our changing times, but the fact that precisely these feelings find expression in precisely this way must surely have something also to do with the inevitability of stage censorship's demise: even before it had actually gone, playwrights were ready to push forward to the limits of what had thitherto been permissible and beyond. The same, of course, applies to the radical mythologizing reinterpretation of history in *Early Morning* and the franker approaches of a number of dramatists to homo-sexuality, masturbation and other facts of life which, being deemed not quite nice, were previously preserved by censorship from the modest gaze of the playgoing public.

It is none too easy to pin down what effect this shift of emphasis, or extension of what may be done on stage, has had in general. Indeed, 'in general' it has had little or no effect: it is unlikely that dramatists as varied as Peter Terson, Tom Stoppard, David Storey and Alan Ayckbourn would have been writing any differently ten years ago, censor or no censor, new permissiveness or no new permissiveness on the part of the public at large. But all the same there is something – perhaps no more than an atmosphere – which seems to give the work of an almost equally varied selection of dramatists – among them Bond, Wood, Williams, Brenton, David Cregan, David Mercer and John Hopkins – some sort of consistency, some distinctive quality which we would recognize as belonging unmistakably to the end of the 1960s and the beginning of the 1970s. The key to it is perhaps the idea of physical and emotional violence – a violence harnessed in various ways, through ritual, theatrical formalism, tight verbal control, comic endistancement, but still inescapably there as a motive force in the writing.

If one were to put together plays as superficially disparate us *Early Morning*, '*H*', *AC/DC*, *Christie in Love*, *Three Men for Colverton*, *Belcher's Luck* and *This Story of Yours*, I think a certain consistency would become apparent. In all of them an anarchic spirit seems to be abroad. Sometimes, though not always, it is an anarchism born of despair – despair at the decay of forms, the inescapable disharmony between man and his environment, the tragic inability of man to come to terms directly with society as it now is, with scientific development, with the uncontrollable forces within his own nature; man's inability to live happily either in chains or free, either with religion or without it. Hence many of the characters in these plays live on or over the edge of madness, and the old standards, if they are not regarded (as in *Early Morning*) as in themselves vicious and ripe for destruction, are shown as totally impractical for the new situations in which they are required to function, the new men they have to function on.

Is this, then, a drama of despair? In a way it may be: there is often underlying it the sense, expressed directly by David Mercer, that humanity has been 'in the wrong bloody boat ever since Plato', and that 'it's too late to roll back the whole history of Western civilization, to get back to sources and start again'. But as against this there are signs of hope. It may be only the rather negative acceptance that, whether or not philosophically speaking we ought to be just carrying on as usual, that is in fact precisely what most of us are doing: the consideration which influenced David Storey, in revising *The Restoration of Arnold Middleton*, to let his hero live on and return to a sort of sanity in the end instead of killing himself. In Edward Bond's plays there is always a Blakean innocent to survive the horrors of what is going on around him, and even if, in the case of Kiro in *Narrow Road to the Deep North*, the individual may despair and perish, the type survives.

Most of the dramatists seem to predicate a hope of some kind by reference to positive standards: sanity as against insanity, natural vitality as against the debilitating forces of modern urbanized life, even sheer middle-class stolidity in the face of any kind of disaster. Heathcote Williams, and perhaps Howard Brenton, seem to offer a different sort of alternative: in their plays we see something which could be interpreted as that other boat humanity ought to get into – a world in which traditional morality of any kind (not merely Judaeo-Christian) has vanished, in which sanity itself is seen as a shackle. Whether escape from our present human predicament into the schizophrenic world inhabited by the characters of *AC/DC* would strike most of us as a hopeful prospect is another matter; but at least it may be seen as a modern answer to a dilemma of which our own age is particularly conscious.

And beyond all these matters of content, there is always the matter of form. In the theatre today it may well be, to use Marshall McLuhan's formulation rather cavalierly to other ends than he intended, that the medium is the message. The very fact that, having a vision of a world in dissolution, these literary artists still choose to express it in the ordered, coherent shape of a written play must mean something. As long as an experience, however incoherent and despairing, can be shaped into a coherent work of art, can be abstracted in order to be communicated, all is not lost. There are, it is true, more and more kinds of theatre which turn their back on this traditional form of primarily verbal communication, but whether or not it theoretically should, the written drama, like humanity itself, keeps on keeping on. And in doing so it still throws up enough new excitements, enough worthwhile new talents, to justify its continued survival and to perpetuate itself. The medium, and its survival, *is* the message; despair expressed is not total despair; the end has not come, and will not come, until there is nothing left but silence.

Bibliography of Playscripts

Bibliography of Playscripts

ALAN AYCKBOURN

Relatively Speaking. Evans Bros. 1969

Ernie's Incredible Illucinations. In *Playbill One*. Hutchinson Educational. 1969

Countdown. In *Mixed Doubles*. Methuen. 1970

How the Other Half Loves. Evans Bros. 1973

The Norman Conquests. Chatto and Windus. 1975

Three Plays (Absurd Person Singular, Absent Friends, Bedroom Farce). Chatto and Windus. 1977

PETER BARNES

The Ruling Class. Heinemann Educational. 1969

Leonardo's Last Supper and *Noonday Demons*. Heinemann Educational. 1970

The Bewitched. Heinemann Educational. 1974

Laughter. Heinemann Educational. 1978

EDWARD BOND

Saved. Methuen. 1966. New edition 1969. Also in *Plays: One*. Eyre Methuen. 1977

Narrow Road to the Deep North. Methuen. 1968

Early Morning. Calder and Boyars. 1968. Revised in *Plays: One*. Eyre Methuen 1977.

The Pope's Wedding (with '*Sharpeville Sequence*', including *Black Mass*). Methuen. 1971. Also in *Plays: One*. Eyre Methuen. 1977

Lear. Eyre Methuen. 1972

The Sea. Eyre Methuen. 1973

Bingo and *Passion*. Eyre Methuen. 1974

The Fool and *We Come to the River*. Eyre Methuen. 1976
Theatre Poems and Songs. Eyre Methuen. 1978
The Bundle. Eyre Methuen. 1978

HOWARD BRENTON
Revenge. Methuen. 1970
Christie in Love and other plays (*Heads, The Education of Skinny Spew*). Methuen. 1970
Lay-By (with other authors). Calder and Boyars. 1972
Plays for Public Places (*Gum and Goo, Wesley, Scott of the Antarctic*). Eyre Methuen. 1972
Magnificence. Eyre Methuen. 1973
The Churchill Play. Eyre Methuen. 1974
Brassneck (with David Hare). Eyre Methuen. 1974
Weapons of Happiness. Eyre Methuen. 1976
Epsom Downs. Eyre Methuen. 1977

DAVID CAUTE
The Demonstration. André Deutsch. 1970

WILLIAM CORLETT
Tinker's Curse. In *Plays of the Year 34*. Elek. 1968

DAVID CREGAN
Transcending and *The Dancers*. Methuen. 1967
Three Men for Colverton. Methuen. 1967
The Houses by the Green. Methuen. 1969
Albert. In *Playbill One*. Hutchinson Educational. 1969
Miniatures. Methuen. 1970
The Land of Palms. Eyre Methuen. 1973
How We Held The Square. Eyre Methuen. 1973
Poor Tom and *Tina*. Eyre Methuen. 1976

BARRY ENGLAND
Conduct Unbecoming. Heinemann Educational. 1971

SIMON GRAY

Wise Child. Faber. 1968

Dutch Uncle. Faber. 1969

Sleeping Dog. Faber. 1969

The Idiot. Methuen. 1971

Spoiled. Methuen. 1971

Butley. Methuen. 1971

Otherwise Engaged and other plays (*Two Sundays, Plaintiffs and Defendants*). Eyre Methuen. 1975

Dog Days. Eyre Methuen. 1976

The Rear Column and other plays (*Molly, Man in a Side-Car*). Eyre Methuen. 1978

DAVID HALLIWELL

Little Malcolm and His Struggle Against the Eunuchs. Faber. 1967

K. D. Dufford Hears K. D. Dufford Ask K. D. Dufford How K. D. Dufford'll Make K. D. Dufford. Faber. 1970

A Who's Who of Flapland and other plays (*A Discussion, Muck from Three Angles*). Faber. 1971

CHRISTOPHER HAMPTON

When Did You Last See My Mother? Faber. 1967

Marya (adapted from Isaac Babel). In *Plays of the Year 35*. Elek. 1969

Total Eclipse. Faber. 1969

The Philanthropist. Faber. 1970

Molière's Don Juan. Faber. 1973

Savages. Faber. 1974

Treats. Faber. 1976

DAVID HARE

Slag. Faber. 1971

The Great Exhibition. Faber. 1972

Brassneck (with Howard Brenton). Eyre Methuen. 1974

Knuckle. Faber. 1974
Teeth 'n' Smiles. Faber. 1976
Fanshen. Faber. 1976

JOHN HOPKINS
Talking to a Stranger. Penguin. 1967
A Place of Safety. In *Z Cars*. Longmans. 1968
A Game – Like – Only a Game. In *Conflicting Generations*.
    Longman. 1968
This Story of Yours. Penguin. 1969
Find Your Way Home. Penguin. 1971

KEVIN LAFFAN
Zoo Zoo Widdershins Zoo. Faber. 1969
It's a Two-Foot-Six-Inches-Above-the-Ground World. Faber. 1970

DAVID MERCER
*The Generations: Where the Difference Begins, A Climate of Fear,
    The Birth of a Private Man*. John Calder. 1964
Ride a Cock Horse. Calder and Boyars. 1966
*Three Television Comedies: A Suitable Case for Treatment, For Tea
    on Sunday, And Did Those Feet?* Calder and Boyars. 1966
Belcher's Luck. Calder and Boyars. 1966
The Governor's Lady. Methuen. 1968
The Parachute, with two more TV plays: *Let's Murder Vivaldi,
    In Two Minds*. Calder and Boyars. 1969
After Haggerty. Methuen. 1970
Flint. Methuen. 1970
On the Eve of Publication and other plays (*The Cellar and the
    Almond Tree, Emma's Time*). Methuen. 1970
The Bankrupt and other plays (*You and Me and Him, Find Me,
    An Afternoon at the Festival*). Eyre Methuen. 1974
Duck Song. Eyre Methuen. 1974
Huggy Bear and other plays (*The Arcata Promise, A Super-
    stition*). Eyre Methuen. 1977

PETER NICHOLS

Promenade. In *Six Granada Plays*. Faber. 1960
Ben Spray. In *New Granada Plays*. Faber. 1961
A Day in the Death of Joe Egg. Faber. 1967
The National Health, or Nurse Norton's Affair. Faber. 1970
Forget-Me-Not Lane. Faber. 1971
Chez Nous. Faber. 1974
The Freeway. Faber. 1975
Privates on Parade. Faber. 1977

JOE ORTON

Entertaining Mr Sloane. In *New English Dramatists 8*. Penguin.
    1965. Eyre Methuen. 1973
The Ruffian on the Stair (first version). In *New Radio Drama*.
    BBC. 1966
Loot. Methuen. 1967. In *New English Dramatists 13*. Penguin.
    1968
Crimes of Passion: The Ruffian on the Stair and *The Erpingham
    Camp*. Methuen. 1967
What the Butler Saw. Methuen. 1969
Funeral Games and *The Good and Faithful Servant*. Methuen.
    1970
The Complete Plays. Eyre Methuen. 1976

DAVID PINNER

Fanghorn. Penguin. 1966
Dickon. In *New English Dramatists 10*. Penguin. 1967
The Drums of Snow. In *New English Dramatists 13*. Penguin.
    1968. Also in *Plays of the Year 42*. Elek. 1972

ALAN PLATER

Mating Season. In *Worth a Hearing*. Blackie. 1967
A Quiet Night. In *Z Cars*. Longman. 1968
Close the Coalhouse Door. Methuen. 1969
Excursion. In *Playbill Three*. Hutchinson Educational. 1969

You and Me. (Four plays: *Excursion, On Christmas Day in the Morning, And a Little Love Besides, 17 Percent Said Push Off.*) Blackie. 1973
And a Little Love Besides. French. 1973
See the Pretty Lights. In *Theatre Choice.* Blackie. 1974
The Trouble with Abracadabra. Macmillan Educational. 1975
Fosdyke One. French. 1978

DAVID SELBOURNE
The Two-Backed Beast. Methuen. 1968
The Play of William Cooper and Edmund Dew-Nevett. Methuen. 1969
Dorabella. Methuen. 1970
Samson and *Alison Fagan.* Calder and Boyars. 1971
The Damned. Methuen. 1971

ANTHONY SHAFFER
Sleuth. Calder and Boyars. 1970

ROBERT SHAW
The Man in the Glass Booth. In *Plays of the Year 34.* Elek. 1968
Cato Street. Chatto and Windus. 1972

COLIN SPENCER
Spitting Image. In *Plays and Players.* November 1968.

TOM STOPPARD
Rosencrantz and Guildenstern are Dead. Faber. 1967
Enter a Free Man. Faber. 1968
The Real Inspector Hound. Faber. 1968
Albert's Bridge and *If You're Glad I'll Be Frank.* Faber. 1969
A Separate Peace. In *Playbill Two.* Hutchinson Educational. 1969
After Magritte. Faber. 1971

Jumpers. Faber. 1972

Artist Descending a Staircase and *Where Are They Now?* Faber. 1973

Travesties. Faber. 1975

Dirty Linen and *New-Found-Land*. Faber. 1976

Every Good Boy Deserves Favour and *Professional Foul*. Faber. 1978

DAVID STOREY

The Restoration of Arnold Middleton. Cape. 1967. In *New English Dramatists 14*. Penguin. 1970

In Celebration. Cape. 1969. Penguin (with *The Contractor*). 1971

The Contractor. Cape. 1970. Penguin (with *In Celebration*). 1971

Home. Cape. 1970. Penguin. 1972

The Changing Room. Cape. 1972. Penguin. 1973

The Farm. Cape. 1973

Cromwell. Cape. 1973

Life Class. Cape. 1975

CECIL P. TAYLOR

Allergy. In *Traverse Plays*. Penguin. 1966

The Ballachulish Beat. Rapp & Carroll. 1967

Bread and Butter. In *New English Dramatists 10*. Penguin. 1967

Revolution: Cromwell. In *Making a TV Play*, by Cecil P. Taylor. Oriel Press. 1970

Thank You Very Much. Methuen Young Drama. 1970

PETER TERSON

A Night to Make the Angels Weep. In *New English Dramatists 11*. Penguin. 1967

The Mighty Reservoy. In *New English Dramatists 14*. Penguin. 1970

Zigger Zagger. *Mooney and His Caravan*. Penguin. 1970

The Apprentices. Penguin. 1970
Spring-Heeled Jack. Penguin. 1971
The Adventures of Gervase Becket, or The Man Who Changed Places. Methuen Young Drama. 1971

HEATHCOTE WILLIAMS
The Local Stigmatic. In *Traverse Plays*. Penguin. 1966
AC/DC. Calder and Boyars. 1972

CHARLES WOOD
Cockade. In *New English Dramatists 8*. Penguin. 1965
Fill the Stage with Happy Hours. In *New English Dramatists 11*. Penguin. 1967
Dingo. Penguin. 1969
'H', or Monologues at Front of Burning Cities. Methuen. 1970
Veterans. Eyre Methuen. 1972